Candidates for Sainthood

Candidates for Sainthood

By
Leo Knowles

Carillon Books
St. Paul, Minnesota

CANDIDATES FOR SAINTHOOD
A Carillon Book

Carillon Books Edition published 1978
ISBN: 0-89310-035-8 (Hardcover)
         0-89310-036-6 (Paperback)

Library of Congress Catalog Card Number 78-552-47

Carillon Books
2115 Summit Avenue
St. Paul, Minnesota 55105 U.S.A.

In accordance with the decrees of Pope Urban VIII, we wish to state that nothing in these pages is intended to anticipate any future decision of the Holy See.

ACKNOWLEDGEMENT

My thanks are due to the Editor of *Catholic Fireside*, London, for permission to reproduce the chapter on Don Orione, which first appeared as an article in his magazine.

L.K.

Contents

I

The Marabout of Jesus

One October morning in 1886, a handsome young Frenchman went into the Church of St. Augustin in Paris just as the
nine o'clock Mass was beginning. He made for the confessional of the Abbé Huvelin and entered.

"Father, I haven't come to confession. I lost my Faith a long
time ago," he announced.

"Then what may I do for you, my son?"

The voice behind the grille was grave yet serene.

"Instruct me. You see, I *want* to believe."

"Kneel down and make your confession," the Abbé commanded. His voice was kind but firm.

"But Father, I don't think you have understood . . ."

"Don't argue, my son. And don't worry. Just do as I say."

Still taken aback, the young man knelt down and blurted as
many sins as he could remember. The Abbé gave him
absolution.

"Now, are you fasting?" he inquired.

"Yes," the penitent replied.

"Very well. Go straight away and receive Holy
Communion."

The penitent, an ex-army officer, knew an order when he

heard one. Bemused, he went to the altar and, for the first time in twelve years, was reunited with his Lord.

In St. Augustin today, a plaque commemorates that morning, more than ninety years ago, when Charles de Foucauld came back to the Church. It also records that many years later, as a priest, Charles said Mass there.

As most people know, Charles spent his life not in Paris but in the desert—in the Algerian Sahara. As a missionary he was not a success. He scarcely made a single convert. He tried to form a religious order and failed completely—his only novice soon left. When he died a martyr in 1916, the news caused scarcely a ripple. On the face of it his death was unnecessary, even ridiculous. His cousin, a general, described him as a fool.

Yet fifty years afterwards, in his encyclical *Populorum Progressio,* Pope Paul VI held him up as an example to the world: a man who, by living the Gospel literally earned for himself the title he claimed—Universal Brother.

Charles Eugene, Vicomte de Foucauld, was born in the beautiful old city of Strasbourg on September 15th, 1858. When he was six his parents died within months of each other. Nevertheless he and his younger sister, Marie, had a happy childhood in the care of Colonel de Morlet, their seventy-year-old maternal grandfather.

Charles was a gay, affectionate child with a lively imagination and a will of his own. The kindly old colonel, despite a lifetime in the army, proved to be a poor disciplinarian. Young Charles soon discovered that a well-orchestrated tantrum could get him anything. "When he cries he reminds me of my daughter," sighed grandfather, surrendering without a fight. Not only was Charles ill-tempered, he was also greedy. At parties he would swoop on the cakes before the other children had a chance, and gobble up the whole plateful.

The wayward young glutton was eleven when his cousin, Marie Moitessier, first took him under her wing. Marie was eight years older, a beautiful young woman with a profound spiritual life and a special devotion to the Sacred Heart. On a long holiday at her family's summer home Marie took her orphan cousin for long walks, just as his father had done before tuberculosis finally robbed him of his strength. Marie's deep piety reminded Charles of the mother whom he had lost so soon after his father; the mother, herself so devout, who had first taught him his prayers.

The accord begun that summer never broke or faltered; it endured until Charles' death. Undoubtedly, it was one of the great spiritual friendships of all time. Yet we know maddeningly little about it, because Marie's letters to Charles have not survived and we only have fragments of his to her.

When Charles, at high-school age, began to lose his Faith, Marie did not lecture or badger him; nor did she when, at a Jesuit boarding-school in Paris, he got into trouble through his amorous escapades with shopgirls. At the age of seventeen he was, by his own account, "all egoism, vanity, impiety, evil-doing". Yet Marie, now the Vicomtesse de Bondy, remained as cheerful and affectionate as ever.

Charles needed all her affection, for he was desperately unhappy at school. The regime was strict and the work hard; the day began at 4:40 a.m. Charles, who was neither lazy nor stupid, virtually went on strike, hoping to be expelled. Meantime, he consoled himself with mountains of cakes and put on weight alarmingly. In March, 1876, the Jesuits gave in. Charles was asked to leave.

At the military academy of St. Cyr he worked hard at first, but his grandfather's death in February, 1879, seems to have thrown him off-balance and his studies suffered badly. However, he was gazetted with the rank of sub-lieutenant and sent on to the cavalry school at Saumur. At the same time, on his twentieth birthday, he inherited a fortune from his grandfather.

His extravagance made him the talk of the town. Every night he gorged himself at a fashionable restaurant. He threw wild parties for his friends. He patronised the best hairdresser, the best bootmaker, the best tailor. When he entertained, he hired all the cabs in town for the whole evening, instructing them to drive around until they were needed.

Of course there were women; many, many women. "I rent by the day, not by the month," he told each new mistress with brutal honesty.

He began to play strange pranks. On one occasion he got himself arrested when he entered a restaurant wearing an obviously false beard and the manager took him for a bandit.

Another escapade is now seen to be highly significant. Suddenly one morning, he disappeared from the school. As day after day went by without any trace of him, alarm grew. A police search was mounted. After nearly a month he was discovered, wandering through the countryside in a beggar's rags.

"I got fed up with comfort and luxury," he explained. "I wanted to feel for myself what it was like to be poor."

Passing out of Saumur eighty-seventh in a class of eighty-seven, Second-Lieutenant de Foucauld found himself at Pont-a-Mousson, near Nancy. There he set up house with a lady known as Mimi.

Now the army had no objection to his keeping a mistress, but when the regiment was posted to Algeria and Charles tried to pass Mimi off as the Vicomtesse de Foucauld, authority came down with a firm hand. Charles was given an ultimatum: Mimi must go. Charles was defiant. The lady was not, he pointed out, subject to military discipline. The case was referred to Paris. Charles was removed from active service.

It did not take long for him to realise his mistake, for by now Africa was in his blood. Living with Mimi beside Lake Geneva, he continued to study Arabic and African history. The more he studied, the more unhappy and restless he became. In the end, he bade Mimi a fond farewell and asked to be reinstated in the army. Charles de Foucauld was at last beginning to grow up.

Gone now was the greedy, indolent playboy. For eight months the young officer fought bravely and skilfully against rebels in South Oran. When the campaign was over, however, he found that he could not face the boredom of a garrison town.

Refused permission to join an army expedition to the Niger, his old stubbornness bubbled up again—though this time to excellent effect. He resigned his commission and resolved to satisfy an ambition which had been growing inside him. He would explore Morocco, a vast territory that was then little-known.

To travel under his own name would be to invite almost certain death, for a Christian European would inevitably be suspected of spying. He would have to adopt a disguise—but what disguise? He could not hope to pass himself off as a Moslem. Only one alternative remained: he would play the part of a Jew. As a Jew he would be tolerated and, hopefully, ignored; for Jews were despised by their Moslem neighbors, and so long as they did not get in the way they generally went unnoticed.

Dressed in the robes of an oriental rabbi and speaking bad French, Charles set out from Algiers on the first leg of his highly dangerous mission. His companion and guide was one Mardochée, a genuine rabbi who certainly knew his way around, but was given to endless complaints and sudden fits of weeping. He and Charles quarrelled frequently and fiercely.

Officially Charles was Rabbi Joseph Aliman, a Russian-born man of God who also practised medicine. He did indeed carry a medicine-chest, but his other box was loaded with barometers, sextants, maps and other instruments of the geographer's trade. For Charles was not simply seeking adventure; he was out to make a name for himself as a scientific explorer.

In this he succeeded spectacularly. His accurately-drawn maps, the first the West had seen, earned him the gold medal of the Paris Geographical Society. Later on his book *Reconnaissance au Maroc* won him applause all over Europe—and what an exciting story it told!

Several times during his journey through the forbidden land, Charles had been suspect. No fewer than four times he had been forced to admit his true identity. Each time, his confidant proved trustworthy. One Arab sheik, believing Charles a French spy, nevertheless gave him VIP treatment. He thought that this would stand him in good stead if France invaded Morocco.

For the most part, however, his disguise was successful.

Once, as he squatted in a dusty square, eating bread and olives, a party of French officers rode by. Some of them Charles actually knew. "Look at that little Jew eating olives," said one, pointing at Charles. "He looks just like a monkey."

Where possible, the travelers lodged with Jewish families, or spent the night in a synagogue. Travelling across deserts, he and his companions depended upon Arab guides who extorted money with thinly-disguised threats. Again and again, they were forced to pay "tolls". On one occasion they were actually seized and robbed, and Charles had to listen while, for two days, his captors argued whether or not to cut his throat.

Soon after his return to Algeria, Charles was in the home of Commandant Titre, a distinguished French geographer, when a girl walked into the room. She was twenty-three, dark, vivacious and very beautiful. She wore, Charles remembered afterwards, a wide-brimmed straw hat.

There and then, Charles fell in love with the Commandant's daughter—or at least, so he thought. Soon they were engaged.

Charles's fiancée was a deeply religious girl who had sacrificed a large inheritance from her Protestant grandmother in order to become a Catholic. "When we are married," Charles told her, "you will be perfectly free to practise your religion. But you must not expect me to join you. I cannot believe."

In fact the engagement was short-lived. Charles's relatives objected that the young lady was socially inferior: her name lacked the magic *particule* of the aristocracy. (In later life Charles deliberately dropped the "de" from his own name). Marie de Bondy, also, played her part in breaking up the relationship, though we may be sure that her motives were very different. "I needed to be saved from this marriage," Charles wrote her later, "and you saved me."

It is likely that a man as strong-willed as Charles would have let even Marie dissuade him from marriage if he had really been determined to go ahead? For now he was a very mature person indeed—as his fiancée herself testified when, many years later, she gave evidence to the Postulator of his Cause.

"At twenty-five there was certainly nothing of the child left in him," she declared. "He returned from Morocco a serious man, more serious than many other men at forty-five. He knew life and, humanly speaking, he had become wise."

Clearly, Charles broke off the engagement because of his own inner misgivings, though what they were he never disclosed. Was he, agnostic though he still was, even now beginning to feel the first stirrings of his future vocation? For not only had his Moroccan adventures made him wiser, they had given him something greater still: a growing sense of the spiritual. During these dangerous wanderings he had watched with new eyes the Moslems, so fiercely devoted to their religion, dropping all activities to pray five times a day.

"Islam shook me deeply," he wrote long afterwards. "Seeing such faith, seeing people living in the continual presence of God, I came to glimpse something worthy and more real than wordly occupations." He had, moreover, lived as a Jew among Jews, and marvelled at their fidelity to the faith of Moses in the teeth of the oppression and contempt which he, in his rabbi's robes, had had to share. When, on their Sabbath, they refused to travel or to perform any other tasks, Charles was exasperated. But he was also deeply impressed.

Whatever explanation he gave to his fiancée, she was broken-hearted at losing him. Many years later, in 1913, they met once more in the streets of Algiers. She was now a married woman, he a priest. Glancing at the red heart, surmounted by a cross, which he wore on his breast, she told him that she was no longer a Catholic. Knowing that he was the cause, he prayed for her. In time she came back to the Church.

She never forgot Charles, never got over the pain of losing him. "He would have been a perfect husband," she told the Postulator, "and so I have pined for him all my life, and I loved him, and will love him until my dying day."

She uttered those words on her sixty-fifth birthday. Charles had then been dead for more than ten years.

His engagement broken, Charles returned to France. In Paris he took an apartment on the Rue de Miromesnil, near the Church of St. Augustin. There he worked on his book, taking occasional walks for exercise. When Marie de Bondy was in Paris, he saw her often. The more he saw of her, the more he began to ponder: "If she, who is so intelligent, can also be so devout, is religion, after all, the foolishness which I had imagined?"

More and more frequently, his walks led him into St. Augustin or one of the other churches of the capital. Soon he was murmuring: "O God, if you really do exist, please let me know it."

He was bound to meet the Abbé Huvelin, for not only was the Abbé a neighbor, he was also Marie's spiritual director, and it was Marie who brought them together. This remarkable priest, a brilliant historian and classical scholar, had turned down a college professorship in order to take an unpaid post at St. Augustin. Day by day he sat in his room, a cat on his knees, racked by pain and illness, yet receiving the rich and the famous, the poor and the downtrodden, with equal kindness and equal attention to their needs.

He had, in a remarkable degree, the gift of looking straight into a soul and knowing in a flash what medicine to prescribe. Hence his bold approach when Charles appeared in his confessional on that October morning—and what a stroke of genius it proved to be! From now on the Abbé would guide Charles as he had guided so many others.

With Marie he began to go often to Benediction. Soon he had a deep devotion to the Blessed Sacrament.

Under the Abbé's influence he made a pilgrimage to the Holy Land, arriving in December when Jerusalem was covered in snow. The conviction grew within him that he must dedicate his life to God. Earlier, with Marie and her family, he had visited the Trappist Abbey of Fontgombault, had been deeply impressed to see that the laybrother who took the children to the orchard wore a ragged habit. Long ago, at Saumur, poverty had suddenly seemed attractive to him—so attractive that he had run away to taste it. Now it began to present itself as an ideal.

"It was you who brought me to the Trappists," he wrote later to Marie, but his decision to join the order was not made in haste. It was not until December, 1889, that he finally made up his mind. On January 15th, 1890, at seven in the evening, he left Paris for the Abbey of Notre Dame-des-Neiges in the Ardeche.

Earlier in the day he said good-bye to the Abbé, who was ill. The remaining hours were spent mostly with Marie. When he left for the station, he was crying.

Were they in love, these two, perhaps without admitting it even to themselves? It is tempting to believe that they were. The thought was voiced even in the first days of Charles's conversion, when someone unkindly called Marie's husband "a spiritual cuckold". But Olivier de Bondy never saw himself in that light. He and Charles were always good friends, though he sometimes winced at Charles's habit of ending his letters, "I love you in Jesus."

What is clear is that Marie replaced, and continued to replace, the mother whom Charles lost so early in life. On their journey to Fontgombault, some people mistook Marie for his mother. "I cannot tell you much happiness their mistake brought me," said Charles later. Whether Marie was equally pleased we are not told. She was, after all, only eight years his senior.

Charles was an exemplary Trappist. Even in that company of holy men, he stood out. He performed the meanest tasks cheerfully and willingly. He undertook penances more severe than those demanded by the Rule. Even on Easter Sunday the glutton of Saumur refused to take more than bread and water. He slept for only two hours a night.

And yet he did not stay. First at Notre Dame-des-Neiges, then at an even poorer monastery at Cheikle, in Syria, the conviction grew that he was not a Trappist at heart. He found the Rule narrow and constricting; he preferred long hours of mental prayer to the chanting of office in choir and he felt irritated at being constantly required to change his tasks.

Most of all—incredible though it may seem—he thought that Trappists lived too well. He objected to the distinction be-

tween choir and lay monks, and he was scandalised that the
monastery employed outside labor. Syria did nothing to
change his mind. He compared the Trappist life with that of
the neighboring peasants, and decided that, poor as they were,
the monks had a better deal. This came home to him fully as he
sat one night at the bedside of a dying workman. The
monastery might be a collection of huts, the meals might be
sparse—but at least the monks knew where the next one was
coming from. They did not share the anxiety, the total insecu-
rity, of true poverty.

By the time he was released from his vows, Charles had
been sent to Rome to further his study of theology. His
superiors, despite his unwillingness, wanted him to be ordained.

The Trappists were sorry to see him go, though some of
them, at least, realised that his was a very special sort of sanctity, not the sort that could be contained by any existing Rule.
"How lucky you are to have been given this unique vocation!"
the Father-General told him before he left.

The next three years were spent in the Holy Land, at
Nazareth and Jerusalem. In each place he lived beside the
Poor Clares' convent, doing odd jobs for the nuns. At Nazareth
he occupied a hut made of green planks, shaped like a sentry-
box. There he often painted pictures of the tower which the
nuns were able to sell. In the evening he would go out on to
the roads and gather up manure, which he then presented
chivalrously to the lay-sister who looked after the garden. He
called this offering his "flowers".

He had arrived in Palestine with a costume which, he fondly
imagined, resembled that of the local peasants. It provoked
much merriment among the Arab urchins, who threw stones at
"Brother Charles" whenever he appeared. In return, Charles
gave them nuts and sweets, offering their scorn joyfully to Our
Lord.

One of Charles' great-uncles, a priest, had been killed in the
French Revolution, and as a child Charles had sometimes

dreamed of dying for the Faith. Now, in the peace of Nazareth, he wrote a strange, partly prophetic meditation. "Think that you ought to die a martyr, stripped of everything, stretched naked on the ground and unrecognizable, covered with wounds and blood, killed violently and painfully—desire that it be today."

Meanwhile he dreamed of founding a new kind of religious order, where small communities would live together in Gospel simplicity, offering help and hospitality to all who needed it.

When the Mount of the Beatitudes came on to the market, Charles tried to buy it as a home for his new order. But the deal came to nothing; a swindling middleman robbed him of the cash.

For the present, though the nuns called him "Brother Charles", his order consisted solely of himself. Naturally this hermit-handyman, with his air of breeding and his perfect manners, aroused much curiosity and soon gossip began to circulate.

"Monsieur, they say you are a vicomte," a Salesian lay-brother remarked one day.

"I used to be a soldier," replied Charles, remaining non-commital about the color of his blood.

That he still was a soldier he demonstrated one evening in Jerusalem, where three Italian roughnecks arrived at the convent and demanded a meal which the desperately poor Sisters were not able to provide. They were starting to get nasty when Charles arrived on the scene in best U.S. Cavalry style.

"Come on," he said curtly. "Out!"

The men hesitated. Charles did not. Seizing the biggest, he flung him through the gates and his two companions after him.

"I'm sorry," he told the astonished nuns. "That wasn't very edifying."

He had gone to Jerusalem because the Abbess, who had the Nazareth convent in her jurisdiction, wanted to see this Brother Charles for herself. She half-suspected that he might be an impostor but, once she had met him, she swiftly made up her mind that here was no pious layabout sponging on the nuns, but a man of very unusual qualities indeed.

In fact she was to play a decisive role in his life. In her, as in Marie, he found a spiritual mother. It was she, more than Marie or the Abbé Huvelin himself, who prompted and encouraged Charles in his decision to become a priest.

"I quite understand your desire to keep the lowest place," she told him. "I see why you draw back from the honor which the priesthood commands. Nevertheless, it is as a priest that you must use the gifts which God has given to you. Quite clearly, this is your vocation. And you have, after all, completed most of your studies."

In August, 1900, he sailed for France. Ten months later, on June 9th, 1901, he was ordained.

His first thought had been to return to the Holy Land, where he had lived so happily for the past three years. But the Holy Land was, after all, full of priests. Surely the life of Nazareth could be lived anywhere.

In Morocco, a country as large as France, there was not a single priest; in the whole of the Sahara, seven times larger, only a handful of missionaries. It had been through the example of Moslems and Jews that Charles's thoughts had first turned back to God. Now, he decided, he would spend the rest of his life among non-Christians, sharing their poverty and preaching the Gospel by living it.

"I want everyone here, Christian, Moslem, Jew, pagan, to look on me as a brother, a universal brother," he wrote Marie, soon after his arrival. "Here" was Beni Abbès, an oasis in Northern Algeria, near the border with Morocco.

Helped by soldiers from the nearby garrison, he built his hermitage of mud-bricks and palm-trunks: a group of low, reddish-brown buildings set around a courtyard, with cells for the brethern who never came—though happily there are Sisters there today.

"Already they are calling this house the 'Fraternity'—*Khousa* in Arabic—and I am delighted," he wrote soon afterwards. "They realise that the poor have a brother here—not only the poor, though, all men."

Being a brother to all proved a wearing business, as Charles quickly found. From early morning onwards a procession of soldiers, slaves, travellers and peasants came and went. Everyone sought the help of the Christian *marabout*, this strange holy man with his gentle, ascetic face and the red heart and cross on his Arab-style robe. For the soldiers he would say Mass whenever they needed it, at midnight or four in the morning. He had expected to live a life of prayer and contemplation, but here he was as busy as any city pastor. Yet pray he did, constantly.

Charles was outraged that the French colonial rulers allowed slavery to flourish without restraint. All over Algeria, in the name of Liberty, Equality and Fraternity, men and women went shackled and children were stolen from their parents to be sold in public markets. Charles thought that the Church should cry out in protest against such cruelty—as Pope Leo XIII had already done in Rome. But the French bishops, unwilling to provoke an anticlerical government, preferred diplomatic whispers.

Whispers were not Charles's style. "One of the things we absolutely owe to Our Lord," he declared once, "is never to be afraid." For him, Jesus was "Master of the impossible."

Whenever slaves sought his help he never turned them away, though housing them was a major problem. Some he managed to free by buying them with money from his family. He also cared for slaves who, too old to work, had been turned loose without means of support.

Though a mystic, living in close union with God, Charles remained a man among men. Invited to dine in the officers' mess, he did not turn a hair when some Montmartre songs were played on the gramaphone. Marshal Lyavtey, an old friend of Charles, was the guest of honor. "I said to myself, 'He'll go out now,'" the Marshal recalled later, "but he didn't. He was actually laughing!"

Next day, the Marshal and his brother officers assisted at

Mass in the hermitage. He described the experience with sol-
dierly bluntness:

"What a hovel! The chapel a miserable corridor, with col-
umns covered with reeds! A plank for an altar! Tin-plate
candlesticks, and the only decoration a picture of Christ on
calico! And our feet in the sand. I have certainly never heard
Mass the way Father de Foucauld said his. I thought I was in
the Egypt of the Desert Fathers. For me it will always be one
of the great experiences of my life."

The old warrior had understood instinctively why Charles
lived as he did. Not all his colleagues were so perceptive.
More than once Charles had to endure the taunts of godless
soldiers and officials.

In 1905, he faced a new challenge. Another army friend,
General Laperrine, wanted Charles to move to Southern
Algeria, to work among the Tuaregs of the Hoggar region. The
Tuaregs were basically not Arabs but Berbers, a fair-skinned
people with a language of their own, descended from Phoni-
cian.

Charles hesistated long before accepting the invitation, but
finally decided to go after he had consulted the Abbé Huvelin.
He well knew that he was going into danger, for many
Frenchmen had been massacred by Tuareg warriors, among
them one of his own friends from St. Cyr and Saumur. But if he
felt any fear, he quelled it at once. In Charles's book, fear was a
sure sign of a duty to be done.

Despite their proud history and dignified bearing the Tuareg
were miserably poor, racked by disease and apt to strangle
unwanted children at birth. Some of their other habits, though
less sinister, were highly uncongenial. Their womenfolk never
washed because they thought it harmed their health. Charles
resolved that Frenchwomen, as soon as they became available,
should teach Tuareg ladies the use of soap and water.

The place he chose for his new hermitage was Tamanrasset,
an oasis close to the Hoggar Mountains where, just as before,
he ministered to all who came. Yet, once more, he contrived to

spend long hours before the Blessed Sacrament in his tiny chapel.

A vivid picture of life with Charles comes from Brother Michael, the only novice whom he ever recruited. He was a Breton fisherman's son who had previously been first a student with the White Fathers, then a soldier.

After waking Michael at dawn, Charles rang a bell summoning him to chapel. Since they both slept fully dressed it did not take long to get there. Devotions began with a long prayer in French and Latin, then there was exposition of the Blessed Sacrament, Mass and silent prayer. Charles himself never ate before eleven o'clock, but at seven he sent Michael out to breakfast on coffee and cake.

Work began at nine. Charles shut himself in the tiny sacristy, where he dealt with his huge correspondence, or worked on his Tuareg-French dictionary. This unique work took ten years to complete, and would have given him a lasting reputation as a scholar even if he had no other claim to fame. While Charles was writing, Michael read, ground flour between two stones, crushed dates, or baked bread.

Before the main meal, at eleven, there was a New Testament reading. They ate sitting on mats beside the saucepan, fishing out the food with a spoon. The main dish was always boiled rice, sometimes mixed with condensed milk and sometimes with carrots or turnips. Dessert, which Michael quite enjoyed, was a sort of jam made from flour, crushed dates and water. Supper was much the same, but there was one course only.

Determined to keep his needs to a minimum, Charles wrote his letters on the backs of old envelopes, which he slit and opened out for the purpose. His "desk" was a packing-case; the constant leaning over it eventually gave him a slight stoop.

When Michael finally decided that the desert was not for him, Charles was not altogether sorry. He found the young Breton somewhat lacking in intelligence, which may or may not have been true. Sometimes, one suspects, Charles tended to be impatient with lesser men, and Michael himself noted that he could be tetchy when things did not go as he wished.

So Michael went off to the Carthusians, where he at last found his vocation, and Charles waited in vain for someone to take his place. One of the saddest entries in his diary is for Christmas Day, 1907: "No Mass, for I am alone." Permission to celebrate without server or congregation had not yet arrived from Rome.

Yet solitude was an essential part of his vocation. "One must cross the desert and live there to receive God's grace," he wrote. "It is there that one can drive away from oneself everything that is not God."

It was not a new discovery, of course. St. Antony and the first monks had sought God in the wilderness long before. Today, the Brothers who follow in his footsteps make a retreat alone, in a desert environment, as part of their training.

It is easy to imagine that for chosen souls like Charles, serving God is somehow easier than for the rest of us: that despite all the hardships he somehow passed his days in a happy haze. In fact, despite that dramatic confrontation in the Abbé Huvelin's confessional, Charles's conversion was a long, painful, step-by-step process.

Once, in the desert, an officer reproached him with fasting to excess.

"My friend," replied Charles, "when you want to write on a blackboard, you must first wipe off what is written there. I have, I assure you, a great deal to wipe off my board!"

He could and did feel periods of aridity, when God seemed far away. Perhaps the ex-agnostic was remembering these when he wrote about the virtue of faith:

"It is nearly always faith which Our Lord praises and rewards. Sometimes he praises love, sometimes humility, but this is rare. . . . Faith, though not the supreme virtue—charity holds that place—is nevertheless the most important because it is the basis of all the others, charity included. Also it is the rarest. . . . Real faith, faith which inspires all one's actions, faith in the supernatural which strips the world of its

mask and reveals God in everything which makes meaning-
less the words 'impossible', 'anxiety', 'danger' and 'fear'. . . .
How rare that is!"

When war came in 1914, members of the fanatical Senussi
sect tried to persuade the Tuareg to rebel against the French.
The Tuareg, however, remained loyal to France, chiefly because they were loyal to their Christian *marabout*.

On December 1, 1916, Charles had bolted himself inside
the *bordj*, the small, fort-like building where he lived at
Tamanrasset. Hearing a loud knocking, and a familiar voice
calling his name, he went to the door and opened it.

At once he was seized by a group of Senussi, bound and
forced to squat in front of the *bordj*. A Judas had betrayed him;
the voice he had heard belonged to a half-caste Tuareg to
whom he had been kind. "It is God's will," he murmured, as
the Senussi, leaving a fifteen-year-old boy to guard him, set
about ransacking the building.

Probably they did not intend to kill him, but at that moment
two Arab soldiers from the nearby garrison galloped towards the
bordj, obviously intending to visit the *marabout*. In an
effort to warn them, he made a swift gesture. The boy, armed
with a loaded rifle, panicked and fired. Brother Charles of
Jesus, Vicomte de Foucauld, fell dead with a bullet through
his brain.

"When you set out saying that you are going to do something," he had written once, "you had better not come back
without having done it."

Poignant words, you might think, from the missionary who
scarcely made a single convert; from the founder who died
without a follower.

But Charles was not a missionary in the ordinary sense. He
did not set out to make converts directly, but to show the
Moslems, already so devout, the life of Christ in living reality.
Who can say what graces have come, or may still come, from
his example and his sacrifice?

And the order, which he failed so dismally to establish?
"Where I sow, others will reap," he had prophesied. Today no

fewer than five religious congregations, three of women and two of men, carry on his work; not only in the deserts of Africa, but in downtown deserts of Chicago and Washington, London and Leeds. Everywhere they share the life of the poor, taking jobs alongside them, identifying with them in a totally new form of religious life. In a Venezuelan jungle, on a Hong Kong junk, tending sheep in Provence, running a dispensary in Benares, in factories and hospitals—even in prisons—these humble, heroic men and women follow in Charles's lonely footsteps. Their work is the harvest which he sowed when, on that December night in 1916, his blood ran out on to the sand.

II

Monk with a Temper

On a warm Kentucky evening in 1885, a young man named John Green Hanning gently broke some bad news to the girl he was about to marry.

"I'm sorry, Mary," he told her, "I can't go through with it. At least . . . not yet. There's something I have to do first."

Mary stared at him, her lip trembling. Of course, it had not come as a total surprise. She had known for some time that her John had something, or rather somebody, on his mind.

"It's the monks," John told her, confirming her worst fears. "I can't get them out of my head."

"Go on," said Mary. If she was really going to hear the worst, she wanted to get it over quickly.

"I've got to try the life," her fiancé continued quietly. "I have to find out whether or not I really have a vocation, to become a Trappist. I'm convinced it's what God wants—that I at least give it a try."

Now Mary was a devout Catholic, but she was also a very attractive young woman with no shortage of admirers. She wasn't going to be anyone's second choice—not even when the first choice had been God.

"Very well," she said, gazing past John fixedly, "I release

19

you from your promise to marry me. But understand this. If you do come out of the monastery, don't let me see you again. I wouldn't marry an ex-monk if he were the last man on earth!"

And with that she hurried off, the tears flooding down her cheeks, while John looked miserably after her.

When John announced his decision to enter the Abbey of Gethsemani, Mary was not the only one to whom the news came as a shock. His family, who knew his faults only too well, were convinced that John would not last long behind monastery walls. For had not John Green Hanning got the worst temper in Kentucky? How could any man be a Trappist if he was always losing his cool?

And anyhow, for years John had not even been a practising Catholic. When he did start going to Mass regularly again, it had only been to please his mother and his fiancée. He had, they knew quite well, for long remained an unbeliever at heart. So how could John hope to become a monk?

But a monk he became and a monk he remained until his death 23 years later. In fact, he became a very holy monk indeed—but only after a great deal of drama. And if you think drama cannot happen behind monastery walls, please read on.

First, though, a word to those whose eyebrows may be raised because, twice in as many chapters, I have introduced you to men who, after a period of unbelief, broke off their engagements and became Trappist monks. Here, I promise you, all resemblance ends. John Green Hanning and Charles de Foucauld were two very different men and were led by God along very different paths. Courage and love they had in common—and so they followed.

John was born in Lebanon, Kentucky, on January 12, 1849, less than a month after the Abbey of Gethsemani was founded. It was the first Trappist abbey in the United States and it flourishes mightily to this day.

Trappist monks do not normally run schools, but because there was no school in the area where Catholic parents could send their sons, the monks opened Gethsemani College. There, in the fullness of time, young John became a pupil.

Day by day, his admiration for his teachers grew. He was sixteen when he finally asked his father: "Dad, may I become a Trappist monk?"

John senior was a big-hearted Irishman whose generosity, a byword in the county, constantly got him into trouble. But he was sadly lacking in tact. "A Trappist?" he replied, looking at his son in half-amused disbelief. "That's a man's life. They don't take in babies at the monastery."

It was a stupid, brutal reply and John senior was to pay dearly for it. At sixteen he himself had completed his apprenticeship as a tailor and was already standing on his own two feet in the world. He, more than anyone, should have realised that his son was no baby but a rapidly-growing teenager who would soon be quite old enough to offer himself as a Trappist postulant.

As it was, he chose to look on his son's ambition as mere juvenile day-dreaming and the slight rankled. As John grew to manhood, father and son clashed more and more.

Four years later, the flashpoint came. By this time, Mrs. Hanning had persuaded her over-generous husband to leave Lebanon, his needle and thread, and his sponging friends. Now the Hannings were tobacco-farmers at Owensboro.

What caused the fateful quarrel nobody afterwards chose to remember, but we do know that John senior exerted his paternal authority and young John, now aged twenty, chose this as his moment of rebellion. As he lay in bed that night, anger seethed inside him—anger and the desire for revenge. Long before dawn, anger had become determination. Half-an-hour later John senior awoke to find his tobacco-barn ablaze and his son gone.

Shocking? Of course. But perhaps we should remember that John had grown up during the civil war and its aftermath. Violence was still very much in the air, especially in the South.

John senior had lost a whole year's crop, and that was tragedy enough. But infinitely worse was the loss of his son.

For nine years the family saw and heard nothing of the runaway. They did not know whether he was dead or alive.

What his mother's sufferings were during all that long time, perhaps only a mother can fully imagine.

As the barn blazed on the skyline behind him, John headed west. Even during those first hours of flight he felt the stirrings or remorse; before the end of the day he would have given anything to undo the terrible wrong which he had done. His anger, which had burned so fiercely only a few hours before, now turned to dust and ashes.

Yet he could not go back, even though his father might forgive him. His pride was too great for that. So John became a hobo, stealing rides on hay-wagons and box-cars, begging food at backdoors. When there were no rides to be had, he walked. At last he came to Texas.

And here, in the Wild West, John Green Hanning grew up and he grew up fast. He became a cowboy.

If he arrived with any fanciful romantic notions about the life, they were soon knocked out of him. Long hours of back-breaking work. Whole days in the saddle under the blistering sun. Cold nights in the open when a man longed to sleep but dare not . . . all this and more he endured, simply to keep himself alive.

Nevertheless, there was romance. Like most cowboys he loved his horse—a friend on whom his life, as well as his livelihood, might depend. And he sang—cowboy songs, certainly, but also, and more often, the songs of Kentucky: the songs that reminded him of home.

Like most of his colleagues he rarely used his real name. Nicknames were more common there in the West, where many a man had his own reasons for keeping his identity unknown. John was, at various times, "Kentucky Jack", "The Kentuckian" or, significantly, "The Quick One" a reference to his notorious temper.

I said that John had grown up fast. Nevertheless, it was all of nine years before he finally grew up enough to go home. What finally decided him? Partly it was homesickness, partly a desire to put things right with the parents whom he had wronged.

Most of all, it was the grace of God—the God in whom John had ceased to believe.

Bronzed by his years in the open, he arrived home to as warm and as tearful a welcome as any prodigal ever received. About the fire, no word of reproach was spoken, then or at anytime afterwards.

In 1882, four years after his return, John's mother died. It was for her sake that he had gone to Mass each Sunday, even though he regarded it as so much mumbo-jumbo. Now, broken-hearted because she was gone, he found himself praying.

What Mrs. Hanning could not do in life, she achieved as soon as she was dead. John realised that God not only existed, He was very close. Soon he was going regularly to the Sacraments, praying always for the mother who had prayed so much for him.

His wedding to Mary was delayed for over a year, partly to observe a proper period of mourning but also because John found himself unwilling to put another woman in the place of honor which his mother had held for so long. That may sound immature, or even insincere. After all, for nine whole years John's mother had not known whether he was dead or alive. Anyhow, that is how John felt.

During this period John paid a visit to his old school. To his astonishment he found that once more his imagination was fired by the monks and the life of self-sacrifice that they led. As a married man, heir to a prosperous farm, he could look forward to a life of comfortable mediocrity. As a monk . . . well, that was true heroism.

Or was it? At times he felt that these silent men, living their celibate lives, were in truth only half-men. Then he thought of the sacrifice which a Trappist vocation involved, and admiration welled up again. The world, for all its worldliness, held the monks in esteem. And the world, he knew, was right.

Inevitably John's period of dithering indecision finally came to a head and he broke the news to Mary, with what result we already know. On June 4, 1885, John Green Hanning entered the Abbey of Gethsemani.

You will have noticed more than a touch of pride in his motive. John became a Trappist because he wanted to be "somebody". His Trappist biographer, Father Raymond, warns us not to be scandalised by this, or even surprised. Grace always builds on nature. Often in the past, John's pride had gotten him into trouble. Now, at last, it was pointed in the right direction. But his problems were by no means over—in a sense, they had only just begun.

At first all went splendidly. The severe discipline troubled him less than it troubled many another postulant. As a cowboy he had been used to early rising, hard work, plain food and hours of silence. He found much joy in the long periods of prayer, in choir or alone. He was over joyed when, after six weeks, Abbot Benedict Berger told John that he was to receive the Trappist habit and a new name—Brother Mary Joachim.

But of course, under his new habit Brother Mary Joachim was still John Green Hanning, still "The Quick One". For the moment he was enjoying a honeymoon period with monastic life: loving his brethren was easy and, for the most part, it continued to be easy. Trappists are generally very lovable men.

But in any community where men or women live together, there are always tensions. Inevitably, someone will irritate or annoy another, often without realising it, simply because the respective personalities are incompatible. As the novelty of Trappist life wore off, Joachim found that he and a certain monk were rather more than incompatible. In fact, he could not stand the man.

The clash came one day when Joachim was sent with a little group of his brethren to work in a field about a quarter of a mile from the monastery. Joachim's *bête noir* was in charge, and Joachim was tired.

The monk made a sign which simply meant "work here". Joachim, for some unexplained reason, took the instruction as a dire personal insult. Eyes blazing, he stamped back to the monastery, his sense of injury growing with every step.

When Abbot Berger spotted him from the window, Joachim was pacing up and down at the monastery gate, gripping a long, sharp hayfork in a way that boded ill for someone. Fortunately, before he could do any damage a porter arrived and Joachim found himself in front of the Abbot.

Dom Benedict was kind, wise and very tough. He saw exactly what Joachim's problem was and he did not mince words. By the time he was through, Joachim was blazing mad—with himself. A Trappist, as Dom Benedict had forcibly reminded him, became a Trappist precisely to conquer his own pride and his own self-interest, and to offer everything as a sacrifice to God. And here was he, Joachim, wearing the Trappist habit and ready to avenge a fancied insult with physical violence! What a fool he had been, he told himself bitterly.

Perhaps he thought that the Abbot had been shocked by his behavior. If so he was mistaken. For Dom Benedict was, if anything, encouraged by the episode. Joachim had a generous nature; he had given up home, fiancée and property to live only for God. He was, as he had just demonstrated, a fighter, a man of blazing passions, a man who never did things by halves. Such a man might, if only he could conquer himself, one day become a saint.

So Dom Benedict set about helping Joachim to overcome his pride and his wayward temper. When Joachim, impatient to get his dishes done, piled up too many and dropped the lot, the Abbot made him write home for money to replace them. Later, no doubt, he returned the cash, but the exercise in humility cost Joachim dear.

Another kitchen disaster brought an even worse penance. Joachim, having burned some meat to cinders, was made to eat the lot. It took him six months—he had a portion of the blackened mess served to him at every meal—but he did it.

Of course, the object of this gruelling exercise was not simply to turn a hot-headed man into a meek and gentle one.

Joachim was, at the same time, learning to love God: to offer his bruised pride as a gift. As he grew in patience and humility, so also he grew in prayer, using especially the rosary and the Stations of the Cross.

But the Devil, so full of ruses, set a fresh trap for Joachim and he fell right into it. He started to be proud of not being proud. Self-satisfaction and complacency, those vices of the virtuous, crept into his soul.

Dom Benedict had been waiting for this to happen, and when it did he acted swiftly—even though he had in the meantime suffered a stroke which left him largely paralysed. Making an opportunity of his disability, he asked Joachim to shave him. As Joachim shaved, the Abbot pitched in.

Whatever Brother Joachim might think of himself, barked Dom Benedict, he was still eaten up with pride. Joachim, knowing that this was unfair, shaved on in silence. He was seething, but he plied the razor with even strokes, his face expressionless, while Dom Benedict went on in the same vein, quite unaware of the anger that was rising inside Joachim like a blood-red tide.

Finally the Abbot made a fatal mistake. He raised his right arm—the only limb which he could use—and jabbed an accusatory finger under Joachim's chin, so close that he actually flicked him with it.

That did it! In a flash, meek Brother Joachim was gone and "The Quick One" back in the saddle.

"Put down that hand," Joachim ordered, his voice filled with quiet rage. The Abbot, helpless and terrified, let his hand fall limply as the razor waved menacingly before his eyes.

"Move so much as an eyelash," continued Joachim in the same deadly tone, "and I'll slit you from ear to ear."

With a vicious dab he removed the last of the lather from the Abbot's face and slammed out of the room.

In the half-hour that he remained alone, Dom Benedict faced the fact that he was partly to blame for what had happened. He had meant well, of course. Nevertheless, he had been tactless and unjust. He had been wrong to put Joachim under so sudden and so great a strain.

Needless to say, Joachim was soon back, in tears, to beg forgiveness and a penance.

"I forgive you, Brother," said the Abbot, smiling. "And for your penance, go to Holy Communion tomorrow morning."

This was, of course, no penance at all but a glorious and unexpected privilege, for in those days weekday Communion was almost unknown even in Trappist monasteries.

The rest of Joachim's story is that of an upward climb to sanctity: not an easy climb, but a steady one. For a number of years he served on the staff of his old school, where he would often entertain the boys with the songs of his cowboy days.

Just how holy Joachim became we may judge from something that happened a few years before his death. Two of his sisters, Clara and Cora, came to visit him at the monastery. With Cora was her baby boy, Lester, who had recently recovered from an attack of pneumonia.

As the three of them were returning, with little Lester, from a visit to friends nearby, a thunderstorm broke. The women were terrified, for if Lester got wet it could well prove fatal.

"Give him to me," said Joachim calmly, taking the child in his arms. And he made his sisters run ahead, back to the abbey, while he walked calmly through the rain. It was a full ten minutes before he arrived, still walking slowly through the downpour was torrential. Yet when he arrived, uncle and baby were bone dry.

Stricken by Bright's disease, Joachim died on April 30, 1908. Even as his brethren prayed for him, others were praying to him, as people do even today. And, as many can testify, their prayers do not go unheard.

III

Out of the Depths

On a breezy morning in 1925, an elderly Dubliner collapsed in Granby Lane as he made his way to Mass at the Dominican Church. A woman and her son came running from their home and tried to carry him inside, but the frail body proved surprisingly heavy. When the priest in his black-and-white habit hurried from the church to kneel beside him, he was still lying on the pavement.

The man was dead. The priest knew it even as he spoke the absolution. The bystanders knew it, also, as they murmured their own prayers. The lined face had a sweet, serene look. Had he known he was dying, even as he clutched instinctively at the wall? At any rate, death had not frightened him; a look at him would tell anyone that. But his clothes . . . his clothes moved everyone to pity. What kind of poor beggar, even in July, went round in such thin old rags?

In the hospital mortuary a Sister of Mercy, preparing the body for burial, cut through those rags with her scissors. Suddenly she found herself snipping at solid metal. Another moment and she knew why the old fellow had been so hard to lift. Round his waist was a heavy iron chain, its links rusted into his thin flesh. There were more chains round his arm and leg, each of them rusted like the first.

Who was the old man? For several hours nobody knew. When he was identified, the details were sparse: Matthew Talbot, aged 69, storekeeper for a timber firm, loved alone in a rear tenement in Upper Rutland Street. Just another lonely old Dublin bachelor gone to his reward. But the chains . . . dear God, why did the old man carry those around, punishing his worn-out body so cruelly? Was he, perhaps, a little bit mad?

There was nothing mad about Matt Talbot—the few people who knew him soon made that clear. To his workmates at the dockside timber yard he was renowned in about equal parts for his common sense, his quiet piety and the ancient derby that he constantly wore jammed down over his bald head.

The derby was more than a head-covering, though. It was also a weapon against the blasphemy which was heard all too often among the rough-and-ready dock workers. Whenever a man took the Lord's name in vain, off would come the hat in reparation. It came off no matter how often the offence was repeated—and there were men who deliberately tried to tire Matt's arm. Happily, there were others who learned to guard their tongues, at least when Matt was around.

When the Angelus rang the hat would come off again and Matt would recite the prayer, ignoring the jeers of the irreverent.

He was at his happiest with the children of the lodgekeeper. During slack moments he would amuse them with stories of his favorite saints and at Christmas time he always had a store of sixpences, which he would first pretend he had lost. A frantic search would follow, until he triumphantly produced the coins from his ragged pockets and pressed them into eager little hands.

No, Matt was not mad. A little eccentric maybe, but a good man whose religion was more than outward show; a man ready to help anyone in need.

Had anyone told them that for sixteen years of his life he was a hopeless drunkard, most of them would have been surprised. Had they been able to foresee the future, they would have been more surprised still. To call Matt a good man was one thing. To call him a saint was reasonable, so long as one employed the word in its loosest sense. But to put him forward for canonisation! How could anyone ask the Pope to canonise a little man in a battered derby hat? Yet the word from Rome—unofficial, of course—is that Matt Talbot could well be the next Irish saint with a capital "S".

Matt was only twelve when he first came home drunk. The hiding that he got from his hard-working father did nothing to cure him. Already he had left school and was earning a few miserable shillings as a messenger boy for a firm of wine merchants and Guinness-bottlers. It was not just the boozy atmosphere that led young Matt astray. Like many another Irish workman of the time, he was a victim of the evil system whereby wages were paid in "checks" cashable in some local bar. The foreman took a rake-off from the bar-keeper, and a man who failed to collect the proper proportion of his pay in drinks might soon find himself out of a job.

Though his father found work for him elsewhere, the damage was done. Still a teenager, Matt was already a confirmed alcoholic who would gladly sweep the bar-room floor to earn a free pint of beer. Week in, week out, his entire pay went on drink. In his sixteen years of hitting the bottle his mother received towards her son's keep a grand total of one shilling.

Though permanently fuddled, Matt never got nasty in his cups—all his drinking companions later testified to that. Another trait which everyone remembered: though he often had to listen to dirty jokes he never told them. He was generous to the ultimate degree: while Matt had money everybody drank. It never worried him that he had paid for the last round, and the one before that. Sure, if he was broke, would not his friends be just as ready to treat him?

No, they would not—as Matt discovered for himself one unforgettable morning in 1884. Getting up with out a cent in his pocket, he waited hopefully on the street corner for a bar-room buddy to offer him the ale that his body craved. One by one they passed him by; some of them, quite literally, on the other side.

So this was it, he thought bitterly, as he turned his footsteps homewards. This was what it amounted to, the spurious friendship of the tavern! Each of those men knew what he was suffering, knew that he was broke. Each knew that had the situations been reversed, he would never have walked by and left them parched. Yet in their own determination to drink as much as possible, they had ignored his need.

He thought with shame of the cruel trick which he himself had once played on a poor fiddler who toured the pubs playing for a few pence. When the man's back was turned, Matt slipped out and pawned his fiddle to buy everyone another round of drinks. Next day he tried to redeem the fiddle, but he did not have the money. He never saw the fiddler again. Then and there, Matt Talbot came to a decision. If this was what alcohol did to men, then he would have no more of it. He would sign the pledge.

Had anyone told him an hour before that he would even contemplate such a step, he would have said they were crazy. His friends, when they saw him drinking mineral-water, could not believe their eyes. Matt Talbot, teetotaller—it simply was not possible. Nobody believed that he would keep the pledge; not his friends, not his parents, certainly not Matt himself. Mistrusting his own resolve, he signed it for a mere three months. He kept it for forty-one years. He never touched alcohol again.

Nobody helped Matt through his terrible withdrawal-symptoms. No nursing-home dried him out, no friend from Alcoholics Anonymous came in answer to his call—that splendid organisation had not yet been invented. Poor Matt had only his own will power to see him through; that and the grace of God.

When he said good-bye to drink, he stuck two crossed pins in his coatsleeve to remind him to pray without ceasing. They were still there when he died.

One terrible Sunday morning he tried several times to go to Holy Communion, but each time he felt himself driven back, convinced that he was about to lapse again. Wandering about

Dublin, tormented by thirst, he eventually collapsed outside the Jesuit church. There he lay prostrate, praying to God to relieve his agony, while disgusted worshippers stepped round him. They thought that he was drunk.

It has been said the Matt's withdrawal-symptoms never ceased; that his body continued to lust for alcohol until the day he died. It may be true. Certainly, from the moment he signed the pledge, Matt subjected himself to penances which would have earned nods of approval from the sternest of the Desert Fathers.

Only on Sundays did he eat a decent meal. During the rest of the week his diet was mainly black tea and bread. At work his lunchtime "brew" was a nauseous mixture of cocoa and a pinch of tea, and this he allowed to grow tepid before he drank it.

He slept for only three-and-a-half hours each night. Bedtime was at ten-thirty; at two in the morning he was up again for a couple of hours' prayer before he went out to an early Mass. He would generally arrive at the church two hours before time, waiting on the step for the door to open as once he had waited outside the pub.

He slit the knees of his trousers so that when he prayed they were bare against the church kneelers and the floorboards of his room. Often he knelt on clinkers lest bare boards should prove too comfortable.

No doubt Matt performed these penances in reparation for his own sins and for the sins of others. But if the craving for drink did indeed dog him to the end, then clearly he had an added motive. Only by such drastic means could he be sure of keeping his body in subjection; of arming himself against the temptation that wafted at him daily from the door of every beer-house.

One characteristic he did keep from his bar-room days: he remained as generous as ever. But now, instead of scattering his money on drinks, he sent every penny to the missions, or gave it to the local clergy for the Dublin poor.

It was in order to send money to the missions that Matt wrote his one and only letter. It was sent only seven months before his death to the friend who usually forwarded his donations for him, and it consisted of these few lines:

> Matt Talbot have Done no work for past 18 months i have Been Sick and Given over by Priest and Doctor i Dont think i will work any more there one Pound from Me and ten shillings from my Sister.

Writing letters, you will gather, did not come easily to Matt Talbot. His schooling had been of the briefest. Yet after his death his room was found to be crammed with the works of Newman, Blosius, Eymard, Grou and other profound spiritual writers; and his laboriously-copied notes showed that he had read them intelligently.

The principal inspiration was St. Louis de Montfort. Under his influence Matt began to wear chains under his clothes as a symbol of his slavery to Mary. The chains increased in weight as the years went by.

Occasionally he himself gave spiritual advice, sometimes with a sort of holy gruffness. When a woman complained that her brother, an emigrant, was lonely in America, Matt nearly exploded.

"Lonely?" he demanded. "How can anyone be lonely, with Our Lord always there in the tabernacle where anyone can visit Him?"

A friend who let bad weather keep him from daily Mass got a succint Talbot rebuke: "It is constancy that God wants."

There was, you will be surprised to learn, one brief romantic episode in Matt's life. It happened while he was still a young man, not long after he had taken the pledge.

At this time he was working for a building firm, and the job took him to the home of a Protestant minister. There, the cook took a fancy to the shy, politely-spoken young man. Realising that she would wait for ever before he proposed to her, she took the initiative and popped the question herself.

"Don't be worrying about money," she told him. "I've enough saved for both of us."

Matt, much taken aback, promised to make a novena to Our Lady and to give her his answer at the end of it. Nine days later he informed his suitor, with suitable expressions of regret, that Our Lady did not wish him to marry.

The cook, whether she knew it or not, had a lucky escape; marriage to Matt would have been gruelling indeed!

Though he became a Franciscan tertiary Matt never seems to have felt a vocation to live within monastery walls. He was perfectly content to remain in the world but not of it, pursuing his fierce asceticism amid the poverty and the turmoil of Ireland in the early years of the century.

When Dublin bosses tried to break the unions and the city's workers called a general strike, Matt came out with the rest. But he refused to join a picket-line and nobody held it against him.

He lived through the Troubles but never murmured against the English—not even when they arrested him and made him stand, hands above his head, waiting to be searched. That happened after the blowing-up of the North Wall hotel, when people nearby at the time were rounded up en masse. Matt and his workmates were quickly released.

In 1923 came Matt's long illness; his heart had weakened under the strain of his hard life. As his letter shows, he continued to think of the missions even as he lay on his back in hospital, saving money for them from his meagre sickness benefit. The ten shillings from his sister in fact came from him. It was his way of thanking her for taking care of him.

Contrary to his own expectation he did return to work in the timber-yard, but only briefly. Three months later, he stepped from Granby Lane into eternity.

On June 29th, 1952, Matt's body was exhumed from its humble grave in Glasnevin Cemetery. In the presence of the Archbishop of Dublin, the President of Ireland and numerous other dignitaries, the remains were formally examined—a necessary part of the canonisation process. Afterwards they were sealed into a new oak coffin and placed in a splendid vault, where his admirers come in their hundreds to pay their respects to the little man in the battered derby who is now a Servant of God.

In a way Matt was lucky, luckier than most of us. He had to be a drunkard or he had to be a saint. For him there was no middle way, no comfortable mediocrity; that option was simply not open to him.

In Matt's day it was poverty that drove men to drink. Prosperity, we have discovered, has much the same effect. All alcoholics, whether poor or rich, need prayers, and generous Matt must have said many for his fellow-sufferers. No doubt he does so still. If and when he is canonised, alcoholics will have a powerful patron.

IV

A Martyr for Mexico

It was the sound of a dog barking that roused her. A second later, fully awake, she heard someone moving about outside.

Slipping out of bed, she crept to the window, drew back the curtain cautiously, and peered out on to the moonlit patio. At least twenty armed soldiers crouched there, rifles at the ready.

Maria Valdes did not panic. Instead, she ran swiftly to the room where the priest was sleeping with his two brothers. She knocked, but nobody answered.

Praying that they had heard her, that even now they were dressing for their getaway, Maria ran upstairs to make sure the route was clear. When she reached the roof, four levelled rifles surrounded her.

"You were lucky, Senora," one of the soldiers told her later. "We had orders to shoot anyone who showed up there."

Meanwhile, the men below had battered their way into the little hotel and into the room where the brothers had slept so peacefully, despite their terrible danger. When Maria reached them the priest, Miguel, was telling his brothers to make an act of perfect contrition. Ignoring his captors' rifles and their sneers, he pronounced the words of absolution. After all, there might not be another chance. Then he turned to the officer in charge.

"This lady is totally innocent," he said. "Do what you like with us, but leave her in peace."

Grim-faced, the officer glanced at Maria.

"Do you know who you have been harboring?" he demanded. "The men who tried to kill the President!"

"What I know," replied Maria calmly, "is that I have been sheltering a saint."

Few would have predicted a saintly future for the brighteyed, michievous boy who was born to Josefa and Miguel Pro at Guadalupe on January 13th, 1891. In fact he nearly did not have a future at all.

While still a toddler he pushed his way one Sunday morning through a balcony rail and tottered unsteadily for several yards alone a narrow cornice three stories above a crowded street. His mother, crawling terrified after him, almost lost her own life in getting him back to safety.

Soon afterwards an Indian peddler unwisely presented the little fellow with a big basket of *tejocotes,* a chalky-tasting Mexican fruit. Young Miguel promptly wolfed down half of them, making himself so ill that his life lay in the balance for days.

The experience did nothing to damage his appetite. As soon as he came out of his coma, he demanded a *cocol*—a favorite bread-roll—thus earning himself a nickname. Years later the hunted priest, dodging about Mexico City under the noses of the police, often signed his letters "Cocol".

There was one incident in his childhood, just one, which hinted at the vocation which was to come. For a time the Pros employed a Protestant governess who pointedly remained silent when, during the lengthy Mexican grace, the "Hail Mary" was recited.

"Senorita," remarked Miguel, "don't you see how only our Faith is really complete? Don't you see how, if you leave Our Lady out, the rest loses value?

The comment was so out of character that the rest of the family were positively startled.

Later, he suffered briefly for his faith at a Protestant-run boarding school, where, refusing to attend chapel, he was confined to the grounds each Sunday. Seeing a lady returning from Mass with her children he called her over to the locked gate and begged her to write his parents, who had been promised that Miguel would be allowed to worship as a Catholic. She did so, and Miguel was swiftly rescued.

Generally, however, piety was definitely not Miguel's most marked characteristic. Invited to become an altar boy, he refused point blank, and as a teenager he once inflicted drastic punishment on a lady whom he regarded as an over-zealous bore.

This unfortunate woman came regularly to the house to teach two of his sisters the art of making artificial flowers. Her real passion, however, was for Thomas à Kempis. Invariably, wax and twigs would be replaced by the *Imitation of Christ,* which the teacher would read aloud with a brio that would certainly have startled the saintly author.

Miguel, pressed to attend one of these emotive renderings, gravely consented to do so on condition that the senorita would agree to take supper with them afterwards. The senorita agreed and the reading—for which Miguel insisted on kneeling—commenced.

Deep sighs and groans soon told the gratified teacher that here, indeed, was a young sinner ripe for her ministrations. With mounting fervor she read on, the noises from Miguel increasing proportionately in volume while his sisters did their best to stop themselves from screaming with laughter.

When they had reached the limit of their endurance, Miguel judged that it was time to bring the performance to a climax. With a loud cry he "collapsed" on to the floor, smashing a small table in the process.

"Jesus, Jesus, the young man is having a fit," screamed the teacher, running about the room like a beheaded chicken while Miguel's sisters, purple with suppressed mirth, assumed, none too gently, the role of ministering angels. Soon the patient had made a good recovery and was wanly apologising for having been so much overcome by the power of her reading.

By this time the teacher, looking hard at the girls' faces, was beginning to have her suspicions. Miguel hastily removed himself to the kitchen to help prepare the supper—in which the principal ingredient was a chili sauce of unsurpassed strength. Of course the poor teacher got a helping that affected her more powerfully than Thomas à Kempis had ever done.

Though this was, admittedly, one of Miguel's more outrageous pranks, he was usually up to some piece of buffoonery. When he was around, laughter was never far away. A skilful mimic, he could and did imitate anyone whose pretensions made them a fair target. He enjoyed dressing up and he had a flair for acting which was to stand him in good stead during the dangerous years which lay ahead.

One day three Jesuit priests, friends of the Pro family, invited Miguel to go up country with them on a preaching tour—an invitation which Miguel accepted with great enthusiasm. As soon as the priests' back were turned, Miguel donned a Jesuit cassock and sallied forth to do a little preaching on his own account—so successfully that the impressed congregation loaded the young *"padre*'s" pockets with offerings of cheese and eggs.

The priests took the jape in good part, though they relieved Miguel of the produce! At the time nobody, least of all the young imposter himself, saw the episode as in any way significant. Why should they?

For, quite apart from his incorrigible clowning, Miguel was a dashing, good-looking young man, very popular with the girls. He played both the mandolin and the guitar exceptionally well and sang a wide repertoire of popular songs. He wrote poems to girls whom he liked and for a while his regular sweetheart was a Protestant; a clandestine relationship which caused his mother real distress when she found out about it. At this time he grew cool towards his religion and did not frequent the sacraments. The mood brought him no happiness; it did not last long.

By now unrest was sweeping through Mexico as downtrodden workers and peasants rose against the injustice of centuries. Tragically, they did not have a leader worthy of their cause: the so-called "revolution" was led mainly by cynical opportunists out to grab power and line their pockets.

When violence struck, therefore, it struck blindly. Inevitable, it struck at the Pros. One night a mob of workers from the mine at Concepción del Oro marched on their home.

The poor rioters, half-crazed by drink, were picking on the wrong man. Senor Pro, the mine's senior engineer, was an employee like themselves; the real exploiters, the mine-owners, were far beyond their reach. But the mob cared nothing for that. Pro was the boss, the only boss they knew; the only one they could get their hands on.

It was not just his father they had come for, Miguel knew that, as he crouched in his barricaded home while the mob outside tried to beat the doors down. For at this time he himself was working hard as his father's office assistant. He was a boss, too. Yet if he felt any fear, he did not show it. To soothe his terrified sisters he sang, played the guitar and handed out sweets.

Suddenly there was a thunder of hooves, then a volley of shots followed by shouts and screams. Looking out, Miguel saw a posse of mounted police hurling itself into the crowd with guns blazing. When they finally galloped away, several of the rioters lay dead.

Did this terrible episode play its part in Miguel's decision to become a priest? We do not know; we can only guess. Certainly, it must have affected him deeply. The men had threatened his and his whole family's safety; that was true enough. Yet he knew that their cause was just and it was with them that he identified, rather than with those who had killed them.

For Miguel never considered himself a boss, or middle-class, or in any way superior to the exploited men amongst whom he had grown up. From babyhood he had played with the miners and with their children. Many a time he had gone out with his beautiful, kind-hearted mother as she took food and maybe a little cash to some suffering family. When she built a hospital for the mineworkers and the government seized it, he had comforted her: "Never mind, *Mamacita*. When I am a man I will build you another."

So much did Miguel feel himself part of a mining community that he often called himself, even after he became a Jesuit, *"el pobre narretero"*—the poor miner.

For the moment, however, he entertained no conscious thought of the priesthood. Instead he continued to work in the mine office, handling the legal negotiations for which he had a definite flair. Then in 1910, something happened which altered the whole course of Miguel's life. His sister Luz became a nun.

Miguel was shattered. Luz, shut in a convent for life—it did not seem possible! Six months later the family were invited to attend her clothing ceremony. For some time, Miguel had felt a mounting fear and now it was swiftly realised. One of the two remaining sisters, Concepciòn, decided to follow Luz into the convent. This was a greater blow still, for he and Concepciòn had always been especially close.

For months Miguel's mood was black, almost resentful, as he stared at his sisters' empty chairs. Why had God brought their happy, carefree youth to so stark an end? But he knew, even as he asked the question, that youth could not go on for ever: that the call of life had to be answered. Soon he was asking himself the next question, the obvious one. What was that call for him?

So it was that at the age of twenty Miguel Pro found himself seeking admission to the Society of Jesus.

The Superior to whom he presented himself was plainly a man with a sense of humor to match his own. To test the young hopeful's mettle, he twice kept him waiting around for half an hour, then sent him away uninterviewed. As he left, fuming inwardly, another priest poked tactless fun at him. When he promptly ran into a band of lugubrious Jesuits loudly bewailing their lot in the Society, it slowly dawned on Miguel that he was the victim of a holy leg-pull. He laughed, and was swiftly accepted.

A serious illness delayed his admission, but not for long. On

August 10th, 1911, Miguel entered the Jesuit novitiate at El Llano.

We have to hurry through the long years of training—during which he and his fellow-students had to flee to exile in California. For Mexico's new rulers were sworn enemies of the Church, and of the religious orders especially.

Twice Miguel was sent to Spain, with an intervening period in Nicaragua, where he taught school in a half-finished building and spent many nights keeping snakes and scorpions away from his terrified pupils. He also had a spell in Belgium, where his superiors thought he would best be able to study the labor issues in which he was so deeply interested. Here he became a miner once more, going below with the men to see their working conditions at first hand and to listen to their problems and grievances.

The Jesuit training did nothing to spoil his sense of fun, which sometimes got him into trouble with more sober-minded superiors. Whereas he had once been rather impatient and hot-headed, Miguel learned to accept rebukes with a humility which impressed even those who were doing the rebuking.

His love of prayer made him a phenomenon even in a Jesuit community. Soon he became known as "the brother who is always praying". When a colleague asked him one afternoon to join in some pastime, Miguel unexpectedly excused himself.

"If I miss my siesta," he smiled, "I may lose my vocation."

"Whatever do you mean?" asked his surprised companion.

"Why, I should be sleepy at prayers then—and if I pray badly, I may have to leave the Society," Miguel explained.

He was only half joking, for though his qualities were obvious enough to his fellow Jesuits, he himself doubted whether he would be found worthy of ordination. His humility, like his love of God, was completely genuine; as the time drew near he suffered agonies in case he should be refused the priesthood.

His joy was boundless when he learned that he was to be ordained, there in Belgium, on August 31st, 1925. His only disappointment was that none of his family could be with him when the great day came.

For some time he had been suffering from an increasingly severe stomach complaint which, the doctors decided, now required major surgery. A second operation was needed, and this time it had to be performed without an anaesthetic. While the surgeons worked on him, Miguel calmly studied his canon law textbook.

His health did not improve, however, and his Belgian superiors decided to send him back home in the hope that his native air might give him a better chance of recovery. Even if it did not, they told each other, at least he would die among his own people.

The well-meaning Belgians simply did not understand how severe was the persecution in Mexico; that in his homeland, Miguel did indeed stand a very good chance of death, if not from his illness, then from the bullets of the army or the police.

When he heard that he was to return, Miguel decided that the rest of his life, whether long or short, would be spent in bringing Christ to his fellow countrymen. On the voyage over he made no secret of his priesthood; he ministered to passengers and crew and when they docked at Veracruz, held his breath in case any Judas should expose him. He need not have worried.

Once inside Mexico he made straight for the capital. Nobody knew him there and he could take the place of priests already driven into hiding.

So began an amazing, scarlet-pimpernel ministry, under the very noses of the police, in a land where the churches had been closed and any priest giving the sacraments could be arrested and shot without trial. All his old flamboyance, all his flair for play-acting, were now pressed into the Lord's service. The policeman on the corner, revolver at his hip, little suspected that the young workman who passed him with a cheeky quip was none other than the Rev. Miguel Pro, S. J., carrying Holy Communion to his persecuted flock.

Despite the years spent in a soutane he wore lay dress without a trace of awkwardness, completely at home in his various disguises. Soon he was giving three hundred Communions daily; one Sunday he gave fifteen hundred.

This sick priest, sent home to die, often had a working day that began at 5.30 a.m. and ended at 8.00 p.m. Amazingly his health now improved—and he even managed to pass his theology exam! Not only did he administer the sacraments, he gave retreats and conferences, sometimes to lay folk, sometimes to fellow priests—"friends in the trade" as he called them in his letters. These were held in garages and other unlikely spots. His ministry was not purely spiritual; he spent much time—and took many risks—in handing out relief to the poor.

There were several narrow escapes. On one occasion, only fifty yards ahead of his pursuers, he linked arms with a passing girl. "Help me—I'm a priest," he murmured. The girl played her part superbly—and the police went scurrying past without giving the "lovers" a second glance.

Another time, he jumped into a cab, shed his coat, jumped out and stood whistling against a tree as the pursuers, in another cab, sped by.

When a police reservist once threatened to arrest him, Miguel eyed him disdainfully.

"Listen, you big lug," he said, "you arrest me and what will your Mama do for confession?"

Mama was a force to be reckoned with, as Miguel well knew. The policeman looked round nervously.

"Look, Father—you know how things are," he muttered. "Please go away."

"I'm not going anywhere," Miguel retorted. "But you are. You're going home to tell your Mama that I'll hear her confession and bring her Holy Communion tomorrow. And let's hope I'll be doing the same for you before very long."

Once he *was* actually arrested. A host of balloons, released over Mexico City, had showered religious leaflets on to a delighted population. Plutarcho Calles, Mexico's strongman, ordered a general roundup of suspected Catholics. Miguel, accused point blank of being a priest, spent a night with his fellow-prisoners lying on the concrete of a freezing police-station yard. His cheerful banter helped him to bluff his way through the interrogation and in the morning he was released.

Nothing, absolutely nothing, could get Miguel down. He seems actually to have enjoyed his adventures and his letters, written on the run, are full of boyish glee. Even when he complains he does it with a smile. After hearing confessions while suffering from a raging toothache, he tells how dearly he would have loved to hit the more scrupulous penitents over the head with the grille. Then he adds, soberly, that many of the confessions make him feel very humble.

His capture was only a matter of time. Miguel knew that. He faced the prospect serenely. Already he had asked God for the privilege of being allowed to die as a martyr, and he felt an inner conviction that his sacrifice had been accepted. Now it simply remained for God tm show him the time and the place.

On Sunday, November 13th, 1927, a bomb was thrown into the open car of Mexico's president-elect, Alvaro Obregon, as it drove along the Avenida Principal in Mexico City. The bomb-ers had been following Obregon's Cadillac in an Essex; in the gun-battle that followed two of them were captured, one badly wounded. Neither the president-elect nor his aides suf-fered serious injury.

The Essex and its driver had disappeared, but one of the aides claimed to have remembered the licence-number: 10,101. An Essex with that number-plate had been owned by Humberto Pro, Miguel's brother. He had sold it only four days before.

Humberto and Roberto Pro, both laymen, were actively in-volved in the Catholic resistance movement—but then, so were thousands of other young Mexicans. Nevertheless they were marked men now and so was Miguel. With every policeman looking for them, it took only four more days to track them to their final hiding-place in Maria Valdes' hotel. Four days later, they were condemned to death without trial.

The press were there in force when Miguel, the first to die, stepped out into the yard of the Police Target School. President Calles—no atheist but a man who literally hated Christ—was determined to show the world how firmly he dealt with Christ's representatives. Cameras clicked as Miguel knelt to pray beside the bullet-pitted log wall. Within weeks it became an offence to possess those pictures, for they had an effect totally unforeseen by his executioners.

A police inspector who had helped to hunt him down stepped forward.

"Father, I ask your forgiveness for my part in this," he said.

"You have not only my forgiveness, but my gratitude. I give you my thanks," replied Miguel. Turning to the firing squad, he said gently: "May God forgive you all."

At that moment, though he did not know it, his sister Ana Maria was confronting the line of guards outside the building with an order which a courageous judge had just signed—an order forbidding any punishment of her brothers without due process of law. She never succeeded in delivering it: the heavy doors were slammed in her face.

As he faced his executioners unblindfolded, Miguel spread his arms in the form of a cross. *"Viva Cristo Rey,"* he said calmly. The rifles cracked and he fell, his arms still outstretched.

Humberto was shot soon afterwards; so were two other men condemned with the Pro brothers. Roberto was spared at the last moment, apparently for political reasons. The Argentinian ambassador had interceded and the younger brother's life was offered as a sop.

In the following year there was another attempt on Obregon's life, this time successful. He and Calles had planned to take turns at being president. Now Calles was deprived of his most powerful associate.

In 1935 Calles was exiled to Los Angeles where he died five years later, still hate-filled and prematurely old. By that time, Mexico had a devout Catholic as its president, and Miguel Pro was openly honored as a martyr.

V

Montreal's Miracle-Worker

During the first days of 1937, thousands of Canadians waited anxiously by their radio sets for news of a small, gray-haired man who lay dying peacefully in hospital at Montreal. The patient was not a statesman, or a prince of the Church, but a humble lay-brother of the Holy Cross Congregation who had spent much of his long life working as a porter at the College of Notre Dame.

For two days before his death he was in a coma, unaware of the long procession of men, women and children who passed by his bed. Many of them were sick or lame, and all of them touched his hands with a medal or some other pious object. Had Brother André known what was happening he might not have been pleased, for he always reacted indignantly if he suspected that he was being treated as a saint. During his later years he complained loudly when he found that some of his brethren were hoarding his cast-off clothing for relics, and ever afterwards he always counted his laundry carefully!

Whether or not he was a saint, the Church will decide in due course. The undeniable truth is that for more than forty years great crowds of the ill and the crippled came to his little room to be cured, and cured many of them were. Even without these apparent miracles, his deep holiness of life would have made him a candidate for sainthood.

Brother André was 91 when he died, but when little Alfred Bessette was born on August 9th, 1845, few would have prophesied such a long life. From the beginning he was a sickly child, a source of anxiety to his mother, Clothilde.

Isaac Bessette, a poor carpenter, lived with his large family at St. Gregoire d'Iberville in the backwoods of Quebec. Their home was little better than a shack.

When Alfred was three a falling tree killed his father. Nine years later his mother died of tuberculosis. The orphaned children were divided among their relatives, Alfred being taken in by an uncle and aunt at Saint-Césaire.

Apprenticed first to a shoemaker, then to a baker, Alfred proved too frail to follow either trade. During her anxious vigils beside his cradle, poor Clothilde had often prayed to St. Joseph, Quebec's first patron, for her child. Now Alfred himself prayed that the saint would help to find him some work that he could do.

Even when he was small, Alfred had been a child of exceptional fervor: his brothers and sisters could not fail to notice how long and ardent were his prayers. As he grew up he began to inflict severe penances upon himself. His horrified aunt found that he regularly wore a heavy chain round his waist under his clothes. Instead of sleeping in bed, he slept on the floor.

Like many another Canadian boy, Alfred heard with wonder of the plentiful work and good wages to be found across the border in the United States. When a friend who had emigrated found him a job in a cotton mill at Plainfield, Connecticut, it looked as though St. Joseph had answered his prayers. But after three years in the States, Alfred had to come home to Quebec. Once again, his poor health had let him down.

Shortly before he left for Connecticut, Alfred had had a strange dream—a dream in which he saw St. Joseph and then a magnificent stone church in a setting which he did not recognise. Now, back in Saint-Césaire, he began to think seriously about entering the religious life.

It seemed a distinctly crazy ambition. After all, Alfred had proved physically unfit for every secular occupation that he had ever tried, and religious orders do not readily take on recruits who are likely to become invalids.

But when the young man confided his hopes to Saint-Césaire's parish priest, he met with no discouragement. Father Provençal knew that here was someone with qualities beyond the ordinary. Because illness had interfered with his schooling, Alfred had never learned to read or write, so Father Provençal himself despatched a letter to the Holy Cross Brothers. "I am sending you a saint for your Congregation," he announced.

Despite this eyebrow-raising introduction, the Brothers remained sceptical. A frail, illiterate young fellow of 25—it really did seem ridiculous to entertain him as a candidate. Two Brothers travelled to Saint-Césaire with every intention of turning Alfred down gently. But when they came face to face with the small, intense young man, they were overwhelmed—especially by his burning devotion to St. Joseph. "I'm sure that if I were allowed to enter his service my health would improve," he declared. Somewhat to their own astonishment, the bemused Brothers found themselves recommending that Alfred be accepted.

And so, in the fall of 1870, Alfred Bessette came to the Holy Cross novitiate at Côte-des-Neiges on the slopes of Mount Royal—the mountain that gave its name to the city of Montreal. Despite his poor health, Alfred had always been a happy person, and now he was happiest of all. The humblest, dreariest tasks brought him joy—scrubbing, mending, washing dishes; all of these he did with the same cheerful smile. Within months, he was given the longed-for habit and became a novice, Brother André.

Not for another two years could he become a fully-fledged member of the Congregation. The year that followed brought little sign that he was becoming stronger. His superiors began to wonder whether they had not made a mistake. Since God had not sent him the necessary health, maybe Brother André ought not to be a religious after all.

When Bishop Bourget visited the Congregation, Brother André seized his chance and made a direct appeal. Once again his shining fervor won the day. He was allowed to make his temporary vows and then, in 1872, his solemn profession. "After all," his novice-master had said, "even if he becomes unable to work, he can at least pray for us."

In fact this "frail" young man worked and prayed with a vigor that would have taxed the strength of a giant—and he continued to do so for more than sixty years. Sometimes he stayed up all night to pray or to complete his tasks, for, in addition to his normal duties, he would often leave the Notre Dame College to visit local people who were sick or in trouble. He ate hardly anything; a piece of bread dipped in milk and water was his idea of a square meal.

By this time he was no longer illiterate; the Brothers had taught him to read and write. He could not become a teacher—his education would never rise to those heights—yet his personality drew the boys like a magnet. Homesick newcomers, invited into his little office for a chat, would soon leave it all smiles.

Two small incidents increased his popularity and caused no little wonder among his young friends. When a new football was needed, the boys were at first refused. Brother André told them to ask again and lo, a new ball was given unto them. When, against all expectations, a picnic came by the same miraculous means, the boys were naturally agog to know how he did it.

"Don't thank me, thank St. Joseph," was the answer, delivered with an enigmatic grin.

Soon, more startling stories were circulating, both in the countryside and in the surrounding district. People said that when Brother André came to visit, the sick swiftly got well. One day a crippled woman arrived at the College; helped along by two friends, she came upon a Brother swabbing a corridor. "May I see Brother André, please?" she asked.

"That's me," said the Brother, straightening up.

"Please, I have heard that you can cure sick people," said the woman. "Could you help me?"

The Brother smiled at her quizzically.

"Are you quite sure you are crippled?" he asked. "I believe that you could walk on your own if you really tried. Why not go as far as the chapel and see?"

The friends who had been supporting her gingerly released their hold. Slowly and painfully, she limped off to the chapel. When she came back, she walked normally.

"When they told me you could heal, I didn't know whether to believe it or not," said the woman, her face tear-strained. "Now I know that it's true."

"It isn't I who do the healing," said Brother André, kindly but firmly. "It is St. Joseph."

Still overcome with gratitude, the woman asked whether there was something she could do for her benefactor. The answer came as a surprise.

"You could pray that one day St. Joseph will have a good home for his Son up there on the mountain," he smiled.

Many a time during the day he glanced up from his work at the tangle of trees and scrubland that covered the mountaintop. Often, in the evening, he climbed up there to pray.

Yet his dream of a church dedicated to St. Joseph seemed wildly impractical. Neither the diocese nor his own Congregation had any plans to build on the mountain, and anyhow, someone else owned the land.

Nevertheless, Brother André continued to pray for a church. Not only did he pray, he began to save up. When the college pupils asked him to cut their hair, as they often did, he charged them five cents and put the money into a little jar, ready for the day when work would begin.

One evening he buried a medal of St. Joseph under a tree at

the spot where, he firmly believed, the church would one day stand. In the years to come many other medals were buried there—tokens of gratitude from people who were cured through his prayers.

For, during all this time, his reputation as a miracle-worker was growing, and some of his brethren became seriously concerned at the flow of pilgrims who came to seek his help. Lame people walked straight, limbs threatened with amputation were saved, the blind were made to see.

Inevitably, the newspapers became interested in this humble lay-brother who seemed able to work miracles, and the publicity proved embarrassing. Parents, suspecting some kind of chicanery, threatened to withdraw their sons from the College. There were those who openly called Brother André a quack.

Despite this hostility, both the Provincial and the Archbishop refused to interfere with his work for the sick. Both were convinced that he was a very holy religious indeed, and that his humility and cheerful wisdom were a sufficient answer to his critics.

No doubt the back-biters would have been chastened had they known of the much more sinister persecution that the little Holy Cross Brother had to suffer. For often, when he was at prayer, a big animal like a black cat manifested itself close to him. Books, glasses, plates and other objects were thrown about the room. On one occasion the noise brought a colleague running. Brother André was forced to admit the truth: that often, at his prayers, he was attacked by the forces of darkness.

When he was a young man, Satan assaulted him with terrible temptations of the flesh—so terrible that he had rolled himself in the snow and done other severe penances in order to overcome them. Later, the temptations became more subtle. "Why should you be chosen to work these cures, Brother André?" a voice whispered. "Surely you must believe that you are a saint."

Brother André, of course, believed nothing of the kind. His cures, he continued to insist, were not really his at all: they were effected by God through the intercession of St. Joseph. Countless times during his long life he hammered this message home. Yet during the early years at least, the hostility persisted. First he was falsely accused of immodesty in his touching of sick people. There were even attempts to trap him. These having failed, he was reported to the Board of Health—who found nothing wrong and paid warm tribute to his sound common sense. In 1910, still a higher authority came down on Brother André's side: Pope (now Saint) Pius X sent a blessing. At last the critics were silenced.

The crowds of sufferers who came to Mount Royal found a kindly but brisk little man whose prescription, whatever the affliction, was always the same: "Rub yourself with the oil and medal of St. Joseph. Make a novena and after that keep on praying to the saint."

As he stood behind the desk in his worn cassock, he rarely looked directly at the one to whom he spoke. Instead he looked somewhere beyond, as though seeing all the world's sufferings. The oil which he gave came from lamps which had burned before St. Joseph's statue.

If, as sometimes happened, a cure was only partial, Brother André was in no way abashed. "Don't stop praying," he would say, "or you might lose what you have gained."

Once a woman asked his help because she was very tired. "Then pray for me," he replied gently, "for I, too, am very tired."

When tiredness got the better of him, he could be tetchy. One Protestant woman was so upset by his manner that she was in tears when she left. Not until some minutes later did she realise that her lameness had been cured.

He had little patience with those who *demanded* a cure. His reply to their "You must help me" was inevitably: "Why must I? Does God owe you anything? If you think so, you had better make your own arrangements with Him."

If he knew that he had spoken unkindly, he was invariably sorry afterwards. "But at least they have seen for themselves that I am just an ordinary sinner," he would console himself.

"So long as they realise that it is St. Joseph who works the cures, I don't mind if they think me a bad-tempered fellow."

Now and again there were incidents that brought his peasant humor to the fore. A woman whom he had observed robbing the college orchard appeared before him soon afterwards to seek relief for her afflicted stomach. "Rub yourself with the oil of St. Joseph," he counselled her dryly, "and eat fewer green apples."

He was deeply moved when a young woman came to seek help for her sister, who was very ill. He knew, without being told, that the girl herself had a serious heart condition.

"Why don't you ask relief for your own illness, child?" he inquired gently.

"It doesn't matter about me," she replied. "It's for my sister that I have come."

Both sisters were soon made better.

Though he spent his life helping sufferers, he did not see suffering as necessarily evil in itself. "We shouldn't always pray for miseries to be removed," he said. "Sometimes we should pray for strength to bear them better."

Usually his cures were effected with lightning swiftness. As we have seen, he could sometimes be less than kind. Yet with one type of client he showed endless patience and would spend an hour or more of his time. Those who had lapsed from the Faith, or were hardened sinners, often left his presence reborn. "Oh, if you loved our dear Lord," he would tell them, with tears in his eyes. "If you loved Him as He loves you. If you realised how sin crucifies Him again and again!"

His prescription for prayer was simple. "To pray well you must think of Jesus on the Cross," he would say. "Surely you can see how impossible it is to be distracted when you think of your Brother crucified?"

Every night, no matter how exhausted he was, Brother André himself made the Stations of the Cross, slowly and with the utmost devotion.

Frequently he had companions, for as the fame of his cures

spread, people came in increasing numbers to pray with him
on the mountaintop. Despite all the obstacles which stood in
the way, Brother André never doubted that a church would be
built up there where God seemed so much closer. And sure
enough, one by one, the obstacles were overcome.

First the owner of the land unexpectedly came down in
price, and the Holy Cross Congregation snapped it up. However, there was considerable reluctance to use it for a church,
as this might look like recognition of a "cult" not yet approved
by Rome.

One day in 1904, Brother André found himself a patient in
the college infirmary. There was one other patient—his
Superior. Seizing his chance, Brother André pressed home the
arguments for a modest church to replace the little shrine that
he had already built there.

As usual, his fervor won the day. Work began in July. A
mason who had been lame gave his services free in thanksgiv-
ing for his cure. At the edge of the building-site stood a box for
offerings—and somehow, there was always just enough money
to pay the other workmen.

In November the church was dedicated: soon it was decorated with the crutches of the cured. Though it was much
enlarged during the next few years, it still proved too small. At
Christmas, 1916, a new Church of St. Joseph was opened, with
seats for 1,000 worshippers and standing room for many more.

Once, when a substantial offering arrived in the mail, the
little Brother had rubbed his hands and exclaimed: "Now we
can build a larger church."

His Provincial, who was feeling a little edgy that day,
snapped back at him, "You'll be wanting a basilica next."

Then he looked up—and saw the far-away look in Brother
André's eyes. . . .

Many years later, in 1922, plans for a new basilica were
begun—the basilica which stands on Mount Royal today. This
was the building which Brother André had seen in his dream
so long before. He never saw it completed, for it was still

without a roof when he died. But that did not worry him for, as a friend in New York pointed out: "You'll drop the roof on from Heaven by your prayers."

During his later years he travelled much in the United States, the country where he had lived as a young man and which he never ceased to love. His fame always spread before him, though he never seemed to understand this. Once he told a friend: "I got into Jersey City just as they were holding a very fine procession—must have been some big local feast." He had failed to grasp that the procession was in his honor.

In the fall of 1931 he had a vision of the Sacred Heart, and then of Our Lady holding the Infant Jesus. They appeared to him late at night, as he lay in his cot.

Soon afterwards, as he prayed in the church, a workman clearly saw St. Joseph's statue shining in the darkness. Slowly it came forward towards Brother André, as though on a cloud and remained in front of him for about three minutes. The workman called out "Brother, Brother!" but Brother André seemed not to hear. Later he insisted that he had seen nothing unusual; he had been lost in prayer.

Until his final illness, Brother André continued to practise a fierce asceticism, living chiefly on dry bread and strong coffee. "Eat as little as possible and pray as much as possible" was his recipe for a long life. Yet when he was entertained to dinner in New York, he amazed everyone by eating every course with apparent enjoyment.

As he grew old, he deplored what he saw as the immodesty of women's fashions and he did not hesitate to make his views known. An offender was likely to be asked if she had come in a great hurry, since she had apparently forgotten to put on her dress.

After some initial hesitation, radio eventually won his blessing, mainly because it was a means of broadcasting religious services. But the greatest of God's new gifts, in Brother André's eyes, was the automobile. He loved riding in this marvellous contraption, which went so much faster than the horse-and-buggy of his youth. More than one driver found himself eyeball-to-eyeball with the law because his distinguished passenger had urged him beyond the speed limit. Usually, though, all was forgiven when the officer recognised the little figure grinning penitently in the back seat.

Today Brother André is buried in the crypt of the great basilica on Mount Royal, in a simple granite tomb that bears only his name. There the sick in body and soul vist him still and, just as in his lifetime, many go away cured.

VI

Angel of Africa

One summer day in 1927 a young Frenchman leaned across the table of a Dublin restaurant and gazed into the eyes of the beautiful Irish girl opposite.

"Edel, I love you," he said quietly. "Will you marry me?"

A girl often knows when a proposal is coming—but not this time. Completely taken aback, Edel flushed and looked down, hating the pain she was about to inflict. Then, bracing herself, she gave her answer.

"I can't marry you Pierre," she told her suitor gently. "You see, I'm already promised, to God. I'm going to become a Poor Clare nun."

A few months before, Pierre, an importer of building materials, had taken her on as secretary at his office in Tara Street. Now he was moving to London, and he had hoped to take Edel with him as his wife.

Pierre took his rejection badly, sobbing his way across the Irish sea until the boat reached Liverpool. Edel, meanwhile, was worried; not only because she had disappointed him but because, under her influence, he had returned to the practice of his Catholic faith. Now, she feared, he might lapse again.

For many years, Edel wrote him regularly. Each birthday,

61

she sent him a present—which sometimes presented problems.

"I am glad you like the tie," said one relieved missive. "I was on pins and needles trying to choose it, because nobody can choose a tie for a man except that man himself! It was the red stripes that gave me spasms. I was afraid they might displease your majesty's taste . . . I spent from one until two choosing it, and the girl was nearly frantic at the end."

A beatification process is a serious business, but those who examine Edel's writings will find many such lines as those to lighten their task and even to make them chuckle. She never became a Poor Clare, but many are confident that one day she will be declared a saint.

Edel Mary Quinn was born at Greenane, a tiny village in County Cork, on September 14th, 1907. Her unusual first name was a mistake; her mother had intended to call her Adele. However, the priest wrote "Edel" in the baptismal register, and Edel she became.

An excellent photograph exists of Edel at four. Even then she was a real Irish beauty, her sweet, open face with its wide-set eyes and firm chin are framed by long tresses. The smile shows a serenity and intelligence astonishing in a child of her age.

At school her teachers soon realised that here indeed was an exceptional young lady—though they would have hesitated to call her a saint! "She was a real imp," recalled one, "never cheeky, but always bubbling over with good spirits, full of life and gaiety and up to every kind of prank. She was the centre of every group bent on fun or mischief . . ."

Cycling at full speed down the hill which led from the convent to the town, Edel would often turn and wave to show that she was in full control. She loved tennis, dancing and playing the piano.

The camera had not lied: at ten she had a poise which many a grown woman might have envied. Instinctively, she did and said the right thing. Not even a visiting bishop overawed her: she chatted away with a perfect mixture of freedom and deference. But poise is one thing, holiness another. It was her family who first recognised Edel's real worth. "Never did we see a trace of selfishness in her," they said later. "She forgot herself completely for the sake of others and she did it as a matter of course."

She was more than bright enough for college, but her family's needs forced her, at nineteen, to take the job with Pierre. Though her sights were set firmly on the Poor Clares, she knew that she would have to work for several years before she could think of entering the convent.

Although she had made a practising Catholic of him, Pierre never suspected Edel's ambition until his proposal of marriage forced her to break the news. At work she was as keen and capable as any career girl—so much so that after he left for England, Edel herself became manager in his stead.

Edel was still a keen dancer and had taken up a new sport—golf. She spent much of her time at a social club, playing the piano and running amateur theatricals.

Yet this fun-loving miss usually heard seven Masses each Sunday morning and was back in church for Benediction in the afternoon. To do some act of kindness she would readily go without lunch, and her mortification did not end there. Soon her life was one long Lent. Whenever possible, she took her tea without milk or sugar and her bread without butter. Breakfast was often an apple, tucked into her purse and eaten on the train which took her to work. Even on the coldest nights, she would not entertain a hot-water bottle.

Yet she never thought well of herself, never regarded herself as somebody special. "I have asked Our Lady to look after you and to do what is best for you," she wrote Pierre, "so you are in good hands. Please do not say you are not worthy, Pierre; it is not true; you are far above me in every way. God knows that, and it is only his merciful love that could call me to serve him in religion, seeing what I am . . ." Small wonder that Pierre, who eventually married a Frenchwoman, named one of his daughters for Edel.

Her regime of prayer and penance was, of course, a preparation for her entry into the Poor Clares. But soon she had a new motivation, one which was to take over her whole life. For, during these years of waiting, Edel Quinn joined the Legion of Mary.

"I'm not sure that she is very suitable," said the friend who introduced her. "She is a very vivacious, light-hearted girl. She might find our work too hard and monotonous."

Mona Tierney had only just met Edel and, as we know, she was not the first person to make that mistake—nor, indeed, was she the last. Anyone deceived by Edel's gaiety ought to have taken a good look into her eyes—remarkably beautiful eyes, certainly, but piercing and full of determination. For a picture taken when she was 28, Edel obviously took great care to look as attractive as possible. Make-up, necklace, elegant hairstyle, pretty dress—all these set her beauty off to its fullest advantage. But it is the eyes that rivet the attention. Their force strikes out even from the printed page.

In the Legion, Edel found that force harnessed: at the end of her first meeting she was totally committed. Soon she was devoting every spare moment to the work, visiting sick and lonely people, praying with and for them, winning them with her gaiety and charm. With one paranoid old woman she would sit for hours at a time, until finally she persuaded her that the neighbors were not really out to get her.

The Legion had been founded in Dublin only a few years previously by a civil servant named Frank Duff. Organised along Roman military lines, dedicated to Our Lady as Mediatrix of All Graces, it set out to provide spiritual help however and wherever needed. Its earliest and most spectacular successes were among the prostitutes who teemed in some of the city's most squalid tenements. The first members braved threats and insults, not only from the girls but also from their male protectors, in order to get them back to God.

After a two-year apprenticeship in the ranks, Edel was herself transferred to this work as president of a praesidium—the small group which is the Legion's basic unit. Edel's arrival sent a deputation of members hurrying to Headquarters to inquire politely whether Headquarters had gone off its head.

How, demanded the protesters, could a slip of a girl in her early twenties lead them in their mission among Dublin's most degraded citizens? Surely they ought to have as their president a mature woman, someone tough and experienced—not this frail Miss Quinn.

"We know her, you don't. She's your new president, and that's it. So, back to work!"

I do not imagine that Headquarters put it quite so bluntly as that. But the message was clear enough. The protesters went, no doubt expecting disaster. They soon found out what Edel was made of.

When two members, because of a misunderstanding about their rendezvous, failed to carry out their Sunday-morning assignment, Edel said little. Later, in private, she delivered a lecture which one offender at least never forgot.

"An appointment to do Legion work is an appointment with Our Lady," she declared. "If you had visited that lodging-house, as you were asked, you might have got a woman out to Mass. And that would mean one mortal sin less!"

She spent much of her time at Sancta Maria, the hostel which the Legion ran for the women it had rescued. She was a great favorite with the girls there, using all her talent for dancing and theatricals to keep them amused.

Yet she drove herself hard—so hard that her friends began to worry.

"If you are not careful," one of them told her as they attended a funeral, "we'll soon be having a Requiem for another dead Legionary."

Edel laughed.

"That would be fine!" she declared. And she meant it.

Absorbed as she was in Legion work, she never for a moment wavered in her determination to become a nun. By 1932, her family no longer depended on her wages. Excitedly, she arranged to enter the Poor Clares convent in Belfast.

Suddenly, Edel suffered a hemorrhage of the lungs. A doctor told her the worst. She had advanced tuberculosis.

The diagnosis ended her hopes as she must have realised even then. Yet she bore it with all her usual cheerfulness. "Circumstances are the Sacraments of God's Will"—Edel wrote that, and she lived it. She went, not to the convent, but to a sanatorium in County Wicklow, where she spent the next eighteen months.

"She made everyone round her happy . . . she would often laugh until the tears came," a friend recalled later. Her best friend in the sanatorium was a Protestant girl and the matron, also a Protestant, grew to love Edel dearly.

Despite her illness, she continued to refuse hot-water bottles and she did not even have many sheets. Nothing could stop her passion for mortifying herself.

When she returned home she was still far from well. In the months that followed her health did not improve, though she obeyed the doctors faithfully. Finally she took a secretarial job in a Dublin garage, in an office so dark that the electric light was switched on all the time. More unpleasant still were the fumes that drifted in constantly through the open door. For a T.B. sufferer, they were just about the worst conditions imaginable.

Once again she flung herself into Legion work. Early in 1936, ignoring the usual protests from her friends, she used her two weeks' vacation to take part in a Legion recruiting drive in North Wales. She returned, not exhausted as her friends had gloomily prophesied, but filled with a great new idea. Her recruiting drive would become permanent: to spread the work of the Legion she would leave her beloved Ireland and settle in Chester, the ancient English city which stands at the gateway to Wales.

Before she could make any preparations, another, more dramatic call sent her blood racing. Edel Quinn was asked to go to Africa as a Legion envoy.

If you think it crazy that someone with her medical history should even have been considered for such a mission, then you are in good company. At least one member of the Concilium, the Legion's ruling body, thought so too. The formidable Dr. Magennis, Ex-General of the Calced Carmelites, roared his disapproval. He had spent years in Africa, he knew the hardships involved. He proceeded to set them out in frightening detail.

When he paused for breath, Edel spoke up quietly. "I know what I am going to and it is exactly what I want," she said. "I don't want to go on any picnic."

A picnic it certainly was not. On Saturday, October 24th, 1936, at about eight o'clock in the evening, Edel Quinn sailed from Dublin on the first leg of her journey to Kenya. She never saw Ireland again.

The full story of her labours in Africa have been fully chronicled by Cardinal Suenens, who wrote Edel's official biography in 1952. In East Africa, in Mauritius, in South Africa and finally back in Kenya, the frail Irish girl labored with the vigor of a Patrick or a Columba. Along roads whose dust choked her diseased lungs, through seas of mud that left her black from head to foot, she travelled endlessly. Sometimes she hitched lifts, sometimes she drove a battered old Ford which she called her "Rolls Royce". Always the object was the same: to set up the Legion where it did not exist and to foster and encourage it where it did.

Once she arrived back unexpectedly at a convent where she was staying after the nuns had gone to bed. Rather than wake them, she stretched out on the veranda and spent a bitterly cold night there, covered only by her thin blue coat.

The nuns, upset, made her promise not to do such a thing again.

"If the same situation arose," said Edel, "I'd have to do exactly the same."

And soon afterwards, that is exactly what happened. This time, Edel was ill when the nuns found her. They had to put her to bed.

"They tell me here that I have vastly changed," she wrote Legion headquarters in Dublin. "Some who knew me well declare that never would they recognise me—except the voice; the rest was different. Also my hair is greying: old age creeps on."

In fact Edel was still in her early thirties, but when she eventually went into a South African nursing home, the nuns thought that she was sixty. At one time, her weight dropped to 75 pounds.

"Avoid everything half-done," Edel wrote once in her own private spiritual notes. If she had a motto, that was it. Though she recovered some of her strength, the improvement was only temporary, for she refused to let up. Inexorably, tuberculosis took hold once more. From Kenya she reported: "I can do a solid day's writing without overstrain, but the walking gets me! After a short distance I am finished and time brings no improvement."

Even when she could no longer walk, she went on writing. Sometimes she wrote as many as forty letters a day; cheerful letters to friends at home, letters of advice and direction to fellow Legionaries all over Africa.

"Pray for me and keep on joking so that I shan't break down," she had begged a friend as she left Ireland for the last time. Edel's letters were full of jokes—yet what she suffered inwardly we can judge from an incident just before she left Mauritius. She had been particularly happy there and as she made her round of farewell calls, she suddenly began to sob.

"Always my life is like this," she told her companion. "As soon as I have made real friends I have to break off and face the unknown." It was one of the few times anyone saw Edel cry.

Her patience, also, must often have been tried. "Sometimes one would give much for a long evening at Regina Coeli just to let off a little steam," she wrote a friend ruefully. Yet to everyone, she was kindly and serene. Never was she harsh or ill-tempered.

As a child she had prayed every day to be a martyr. In Africa she suffered a long, slow martyrdom, joyfully undertaken.

It ended at Nairobi, in the garden of a convent, on the eve-

ning of May 12, 1944. Earlier in the day Edel had tried on a
new dressing-gown with real pleasure and she spent a quiet
afternoon sitting out in a deck-chair. At 6.15 she suddenly
collapsed.

She had known that she would die before long, but now that
the moment had come, it seemed to take her by surprise. "Is
Jesus coming?" she asked the Mother Superior, bewildered.
When the priest arrived to anoint her, she smiled. By that time
she could no longer speak. The nuns carried her to her room
and placed the Legion statue of Our Lady beside her. There,
soon afterwards, the end came.

For her burial in the missionaries' cemetery, the Sisters of
the Precious Blood, who had looked after her, dressed her in
their own habit. Edel, who had wanted so much to become a
nun, became one in death.

Her gravestone speaks warmly of her devotion and courage. It says, truly, that the Legion of Mary and Africa will be
forever in her debt. Yet, years before, Edel had written an even
better epitaph for herself:

"We have only this life, and perhaps only a short one, in
which to prove our love."

VII

Son of Providence

On a railway station at Tortona, Northern Italy, a poor man shivered in rags that were not much use in a temperature 30 degrees below freezing point.

To his immense surprise, he was approached by a priest who suddenly handed him—a pair of trousers!

"Here, my friend," said the priest, "take these; they'll keep you warm."

"Thank you, Father," the man stammered. "But where did you . . ."

"They are my own," said the priest. "I have just taken them off."

And he went off happily, trouserless underneath his cassock.

The priest was Don Orione, founder of the Sons of Divine Providence. The story illustrates, perhaps better than any other, the superbly practical and humble quality of his love for the poor. Whenever Don Orione set out to help, his actions were swift and right on the target.

This same spirit marks the work of his Congregation which has grown with great rapidity, although Don Orione died less than forty years ago, his sons and daughters—priests, nuns and brothers, today care for the poor, the sick, the old, the blind and the disabled on five continents. No task is too difficult or too menial for them.

Luigi Orione was born in Northern Italy in 1872. He was thirteen years old when he jogged off in the little family cart to join the Franciscans at Voghera. He was about to be clothed with the habit, some months later, when he was taken suddenly ill with pneumonia and appeared to be dying.

He eventually recovered, but the superior of the friary decided that Luigi's health would not stand up to the severe life of the order; so the boy returned to his parents' home at Pontcurone.

He was, needless to say, acutely disappointed that God apparently did not want him to become a Franciscan; but this feeling was soon replaced by confidence that he would be guided to the work in which his zeal and fervour would find their greatest fulfilment.

It was not long before God got things moving. Through the good offices of his parish priest, Luigi went off to Turin to become a pupil of Don Bosco, known to us now, of course, as St. John Bosco.

As might be expected, this meeting with the saint had a profound effect upon Luigi, who profited greatly from Don Bosco's friendship and wise spiritual direction.

Like many another youngster, Luigi went through a period of scruples, and once filled three exercise books with his sins, real and imaginary. These he nervously took to Don Bosco, wondering what the priest would say about this fearful list.

Don Bosco looked at Luigi for a moment, then, before the boy could say a word, held out his hand, saying: "Well, give me these sins of yours!"

He took each of the three books in turn, and each one he tore in two without so much as glancing at the contents. "There!" he said, "you have made your confession, now. Don't think any more about what you have written—and *don't* worry about the past."

After Don Bosco died, Luigi wished to give the crowds who had come to venerate the saint some relic to take home with them. So he cut some bread into small pieces, touched Don

Bosco's body with them and distributed them to the people. Whilst slicing the bread he cut one of his fingers deeply. Luigi then did what to him seemed to be perfectly natural in the circumstances—he placed the injured finger on Don Bosco's right hand, then resumed his work. The injury healed completely.

In 1889, Luigi entered the seminary at Tortona to study for the secular priesthood. As he was too poor to pay the full fees, he worked as assistant sacristan at the cathedral. During this period he would eat scraps of bread which had fallen from the refectory table and humiliate himself in other ways.

It was at Tortona, too, that Luigi founded his spiritual life on four great loves: Christ, the Holy Father, souls, and Our Blessed Lady.

One day there occurred an incident which really marked the beginning of his life's work. He went into the sacristy to find a little boy who was very upset because he had been turned out of class for misbehaving and for failing to learn a catechism lesson. Between sobs, the child told Luigi that he would not go to classes again.

Luigi took him to his own room in the tower of the cathedral and carefully taught him the catechism lesson which had caused the trouble. The two became fast friends, and soon the lad was a daily visitor.

Then some of his friends began to come too; and soon there was an unofficial boys' club with games, singing and gymnastics, as well as catechism.

When the number grew to 100, the cathedral canons decided that the time had come to discourage Luigi, so they reduced his already meagre wages.

When the Bishop heard about it, however, he took a totally different view. He placed the garden of his own residence at the disposal of Luigi and his boys—just the encouragement that Luigi needed.

On July 3rd, 1892, the unofficial club became official—the first of many and the foundation of the great work which is today done by the Sons of Divine Providence.

Straight away Luigi turned his attention to a problem that

was causing him a good deal of pain: the shortage of priests in Northern Italy at that time. In October of the following year, he opened a college to give a preparatory education to boys who intended to study for the priesthood.

Remember, Luigi himself was not yet a priest: it was not until April 13th, 1895 (Holy Saturday), that he was ordained by Bishop Bandi, who had so kindly helped him with the boys' club. On the following day, Luigi—now Don Orione—celebrated his first Mass. All his boys were there.

Several priests joined the new congregation; their help was of untold value during the formative years.

Like St. John Bosco, Don Orione was ready and willing to use the most up-to-date means to further his work for Our Lord and soon he had founded a magazine which proved a great success.

A copy of it was seen by the Bishop of Noto, in Sicily, who was impressed with the aims and efforts of the congregation and wrote to offer Don Orione a house that would accommodate 60 students. Here was the beginning of an expansion which is now, of course, world-wide.

Most people who met Don Orione seem to have been immediately impressed with his holiness and his immense love of his fellow-men. A woman once saw him comforting poor peasants stricken by an earthquake. He was carrying an infant on each arm. She at once felt, despite the death and destruction before her eyes, that Love was nevertheless at the bottom of all things.

A distinguished doctor who happened to enter a railway carriage where Don Orione was reading his breviary, knew without being introduced who the priest was. As a matter of fact, the doctor had been looking for him. Don Orione, for his part, knew without being told that something was troubling the doctor.

"My son, who is nearly 15, has been ill for three years," he told the priest. "He can't walk and is in such a bad way that he sometimes begs to die. Please pray for him."

"My dear doctor, have faith," Don Orione replied. "This

evening I will say a prayer to Our Lady. I will get my orphans to pray as well, and tomorrow I will remember him again at Mass. Your son will walk—you can be sure of it."

A day later the boy was cured.

Along with his great holiness, Don Orione had a sense of humor which he did not hesitate to display to Our Lady.

One day at Tortona the food had run out and there was a bill which had to be paid there and then. He went into the church next door, where there was a statue of the Madonna which he himself had put there.

"Holy Mother," he prayed, "at least pay for your lodging!" He got up and went into the sacristy. There were two ladies waiting for him—to give him the money which he needed.

Ignazio Silone, the world-famous Italian writer, tells how he was travelling as a boy of fourteen in the care of Don Orione when the train stopped at Rome. Even then young Silone had left-wing views, and he cynically asked the priest to buy him a copy of a socialist paper hostile to the Church.

With a smile, Don Orione got out and bought the paper, giving it to the boy. Their friendship lasted for a lifetime.

At the request of St. Pius X, Don Orione served for a time as Vicar-General of Messina, Sicily. One day he arrived at an official banquet dressed in new clothes.

"Where did you steal those from?" a friend asked him.

"Ssh!" he replied, "I borrowed them from four different people. If I had come wearing my own cloak, shoes and hat, you would have thrown me out like the man in the Gospel."

On one occasion, he was preaching in a village where drought threatened the crops. The sun was beating down relentlessly and there seemed no sign at all of a break in the weather.

Don Orione urged the people to pray hard, promising them that if they did so, it would surely rain. Almost as he spoke, a small cloud appeared on the horizon—a cloud which grew and grew. A few minutes later, down came the rain!

"We are the Jesuits of the poor," said Don Orione, who died in 1940, of himself and his new Congregation. By this he meant that they were to work for society's unfortunates with the energy, efficiency and total dedication which characterises the Society of Jesus.

When he spoke of the poor, he did not merely mean the Catholic poor. "I have opened my arms and my heart," he said, "to the healthy and to the sick of every age, every religion, every nationality."

Today, those who follow him do the same.

VIII

Saint on a Soap-Box

London's Hyde Park, on a Sunday in 1943. From the Catholic Evidence Guild platform, an elderly Dominican makes an announcement to the open-air audience.

"I am sorry, but I shall not be able to conduct the Stations of the Cross for you this Good Friday. You see, I am going to die soon."

The words are spoken quietly, almost casually. The audience, Catholics and hecklers alike, are stunned. Some of them quite simply refuse to believe what they have heard.

"Father McNabb, surely, there's some mistake," says his favorite Jewish heckler. "You can't mean what you are saying."

"It is true," Father Vincent McNabb assures him calmly. "I am going to die, perhaps in a week, perhaps in a fortnight."

He has, he explains, got cancer of the throat and the doctors can do nothing more. "In any case," he adds cheerfully, "I am an old man."

In fact Father Vincent *did* conduct the Good Friday Stations. He did not die until the following June, three weeks before his 75th birthday. "I don't propose to take death lying down," he declared, and he did not. He spoke in Hyde Park, he carried out his parish duties, he gave interviews to newspapers on the subject of his approaching end.

When he knew that the time was near, he gave detailed instructions to a young colleague about his funeral. His coffin, of plain deal, was to be carried to the cemetery on the back of a builder's truck.

"I know what people will say. They'll say it's McNabb and his tomfoolery—it's just another of his stunts. But it isn't that. It's my last sermon," he declared.

Though he got the coffin of his choice, his superiors vetoed the truck. Vincent McNabb went to his grave in a conventional hearse.

His dying remark shows how well he understood his critics. "To me he was not a saint but a poseur . . . just a mass of eccentricities," wrote a fellow Dominican after his death. Another remarked to me drily: "If Vincent gets canonised, there's hope for us all!"

Yet seven years after Vincent died, Mr. Edward Siderman, the Jewish heckler I mentioned earlier, published a book of recollections about him. He called it *A Saint in Hyde Park*.

"Ah," you may be saying, "Mr. Siderman knew him only on Sunday afternoons. His fellow Dominicans had to live with him." Indeed. But by no means all would have sided with the two whom I have just quoted. Some certainly thought Mr. Siderman nearer the mark.

Saint, buffoon—or both? As long as there are people alive who remember Vincent McNabb, the argument goes on.

He was born, the seventh of eleven children, at Portaferry, Northern Ireland, on July 7, 1868. His baptismal name was Joseph and throughout his life he retained a strong devotion to his patron.

As all the world knows, Northern Ireland is a tough place for a Catholic youngster to grow up in, especially if he is poor. The McNabbs were extremely poor, yet, thanks to their strong Faith, also very happy. "Holy Mass was the center of our day," recalled Vincent later. "The love of it was in our very blood."

His father was a stern sea captain, often away from home.

His mother, Ann, was gentle but nevertheless a woman of exceptional character. As a girl she emigrated to New York, worked as a dressmaker, and was soon in demand among rich wives. When her employer's son proposed marriage, however, she turned him down and went home to Ireland, afraid that a prosperous life in the States might endanger her faith. Her son inherited her horror of riches and kept it to the end of his days.

From the beginning, Joe was not strong. When two doctors told his mother that he would not survive a spinal complaint, she took him to a third, who cured him in two years. In later life he was often called an exhibitionist; probably he became so through growing up, a sickly child, among rumbustious older brothers.

Argumentative he certainly was. One evening his father, hearing the boys quarrelling loudly, came to see what it was all about.

"Joe says he could become President of the United States," the others explained, "and we say he couldn't because he wasn't born there."

"Joe, you know your brothers are right, so why are you arguing?" demanded Captain McNabb.

"I could become the President," replied Joe smugly, "if God wished it."

But he was, too, a deeply affectionate youngster. Even at the end of his life, he remembered the day when, at the age of six, he was suddenly hit in the face by a boy he had thought his best pal. "Something seemed to go dead inside me," he recalled. "Perhaps it has never come to life again."

At first Joe intended to become a secular priest; but before he could enter a seminary the family moved to Newcastle-on-Tyne in England, where there was a large Dominican parish. Soon Joe knew that it was in the Order of Preachers that his future lay. At seventeen, Joe McNabb became Brother Vincent.

"I went into the religious life because it seemed the easiest way of avoiding eternal punishment," he wrote later. "As I didn't want to go to Hell, I went to Woodchester."

They were golden days at the novitiate in the Gloucester-
shire countryside. One day, his novice-master took him for a
walk and explained religious obedience—evidently with some
success. Vincent recalled: "Afterwards I thought to myself,
'That's good. Isn't this a marvellous thing, this idea of
obedience?'"

Obedience did nothing to curb his boyish exuberance, nor
did ordination. Villagers soon ceased to be surprised at the
mad young priest who rode a cycle without brakes down a
one-in-six hill and finished up in a hedge, or who jousted in
knightly fashion against one of his brethren, each with a small
boy mounted on his back.

Long before the Dominicans settled there, Woodchester had
been visited by Blessed Dominic Barberi, the Italian priest
who received John Henry Newman into the Church. He got a
mocking reception and, according to legend, laid a curse on
the village so that no Catholic family ever came to live in it.

When he heard the story, Vincent decided that enough was
enough: Woodchester had now expiated its rudeness to the
saintly Passionist. Armed with holy water and flanked by aco-
lytes, he marched through the streets sprinkling vigorously
right and left. Sure enough, a Catholic leaven soon appeared in
the Protestant lump.

But if Vincent was making a name as an eccentric he was
also making one as a teacher and a preacher, for he had an
incisive brain and a profound knowledge both of the Bible and
of St. Thomas Aquinas, whose works he helped to translate
into English. He gained the degree of Master of Sacred Theology, the highest granted by his order. Vincent would perhaps
have been happiest as a great Dominican scholar, working
among the books and manuscripts that he loved so much. But
he loved people more, and it was among people that his vocation lay.

During the earlier years of his priesthood he served several
communities, sometimes as prior. He was not an easy superior,
partly because he demanded the best from everyone, himself
included. At Leicester, where he was parish priest for a time,

he reacted typically when he learned that the St. Vincent de Paul Society had a small balance in hand. "I hope and pray that there will soon be a deficit," he chided the abashed members gently.

During his Leicester period, in 1913, he went to the United States to raise funds for the new church which the Dominicans were building in the English city. On the voyage across the Atlantic, his fellow-passengers elected him concert chairman. In his element, he regaled them with comic songs.

"Curiously enough New York does not give me the idea of hustle," he wrote home. "It has an almost opposite atmosphere of regularity and decorum."

His mission was, however, not a success. A month's preaching netted only $450 and soon he was on his way home, having concluded sadly that "the McNabbs were not meant to be beggars".

It was during his time at Leicester, also, that a group of women tertiaries put themselves under his spiritual direction. In due course they adopted the Carmelite rule, set up a community and emigrated to the United States, where they now have several houses.

In 1920 Vincent returned to the Dominicans' London parish at Haverstock Hill, where he had worked briefly some years before. Here he remained until his death and here, his admirers believe, he reached very great heights of holiness indeed.

He did not, of course, reach them easily. All his life Vincent McNabb fought a mighty battle with himself, and it was because he fought it publicly that he was so often called poseur, play-actor, exhibitionist.

Perhaps his biggest temptation was to intellectual arrogance. The boy who quarrelled with his brothers still could not bear to lose an argument. Once, when the London community was entertaining a distinguished Redemptorist, an argument blew up about the use of the term "Roman Catholic". The Redemptorist held that it was offensive, a Protestant jibe implying that the Church was an alien body. Vincent took the contrary view. The words "Roman" and "Catholic" were, he declared, part of the Church's official title; therefore the description was proper.

The argument grew heated, most of the Dominicans siding with the guest. Finally, flushed with anger, Vincent jumped up. "You're wrong—you're all wrong," he yelled, and stamped out of the room. The following day, overcome with remorse, he publicly asked forgiveness of his brethren and, as prescribed in the Rule, prostrated himself in penance before them.

Preaching in a fashionable London church, he got on to the subject of Protestant errors. Somewhat carried away by his own rhetoric, he stopped suddenly and clapped a hand to his mouth.

"Oh, my God—I have been uncharitable," he cried in horror. Begging pardon of his congregation, he there and then knelt with his face to the altar and asked God's forgiveness for his shortcomings towards the separated brethren.

On the other hand, he was merciless in denouncing evil. Invited to a eugenists' meeting, he listened quietly to the speeches and then rose to make his own. "You have been advocating the sterilisation of moral degenerates," he said. "Well, I am a moral expert, and I certify *you* as moral degenerates. Good afternoon."

At Catholic Evidence Guild meetings he never lost his temper whatever the provocation, nor did he show anger or irritation towards even the rudest hecklers. One heckler, however, did upset his equilibrium: he called Vincent a liar. Vincent, deeply wounded, got down from the platform and walked away.

On the following Sunday, when he arrived at the pitch, the heckler was waiting. Vincent walked straight up to him, apologised for his anger of the previous week, then knelt down and kissed his feet. Ignoring alike the shouts of "play-actor" from his opponents, and the embarrassment of his fellow-speakers, he mounted the platform and delivered his lecture in sparkling style.

Often, when the heckling was rough, Catholics in the crowd

would become incensed. As every CEG speaker knows, this is a particularly difficult situation to handle, one that can easily explode into violence if not controlled quickly. Vincent was particularly adept at cooling tempers.

"Questioners are our guests," he would say, "and they have a right to disagree with us. Many of you will learn more about your religion from these questions and answers than you have done at school or at church."

As Vincent himself observed, it was not generally the devout who caused the trouble. Some Catholics only seem to remember their Faith when they hear it attacked.

Once, when a lapsed Catholic was particularly offensive, Vincent begged his outraged co-religionists to pray for him—and for themselves, that they might not go the same way. "The Faith is hard to gain but easy to lose," he told them. "Even I could lose it, so pray for me, too!"

Some of the crowd must have smiled at that prospect, but in fact, though he was sure of his Faith, Vincent was never sure of himself. When Cardinal Griffin visited the friars he asked jocularly: "Father Vincent, what would you do if the Reds descended on Haverstock Hill?"

"Your Eminence, I should apostatise at once," replied Vincent.

Everyone, including the Cardinal, roared with laughter. Vincent did not laugh.

Yet nobody proclaimed his Faith more joyfully or confidently. "I have a Catholic heart, a Rationalist head, and a Protestant stomach," he would tell his audiences to their delight, and he insisted that it was his Rationalist head that kept him in the Church.

His stomach indeed protested too much and he also suffered badly from migraine; yet he would insist on carrying out his duties even when so ill he could hardly stand. Despite his eccentricity he had a horror of "singularity"—of being treated in any way differently from his brethren. He suffered agonies when his Prior, noticing that kippers upset him, ordered that he should be served boiled eggs instead.

Self-pity he could not stand, in himself or in others. A colleague, sleepless with worry, came to his room one night and
announced: "I'm afraid I'm going to die."

"My dear Father," replied Vincent, "if you are to be worthy
of our dear Lord you must try to overcome these fears. Now, if
you are really going to die, please go to your room and do it."

The priest did not die. As he later admitted, he began to feel
better from that moment.

Yet this same Vincent McNabb showed the utmost patience
with a senile colleague whom others found exceptionally trying. No matter how busy, he never missed a nightly game of
checkers with the old man, and somehow he always contrived
to let him win.

Nor was his charity confined to his brethren. A district nurse,
visiting a bed-ridden parishioner, asked a neighbor whether
anyone else had called. "Only that old woman who comes to
scrub her floors," she was told. The "old woman" was Vincent,
who arrived in the dim morning light dressed in his habit to
clean up and make tea for the invalid.

Wherever he went Vincent wore his habit; he did not possess
a suit. Since he walked everywhere he attracted much attention from passing urchins, who were apt to shout "Gandhi"
after him.

Though he could, and did, outwalk many a younger man, he
did not do it simply to keep fit. A friend of Chesterton and
Belloc, he sympathised strongly with the Distributist gospel of
self-supporting rural existence and blamed the industrial revolution for driving men from God.

"My dear Parent," he wrote once in a magazine, "never send
your son to a school whose headmaster replies to you with a
typewriter. The God of Abraham, Isaac and Jacob cursed the
men who put their trust in chariots and horses. What will be
His attitude to a teacher who trusts in a *machine?* He may tell
you that his school has an efficient system of central heating.
So has Hell!"

His large, hand-made boots added to the eccentricity of his
appearance; his hand-woven habit he always washed himself,

with much splashing but little success. Its blotches made many a housewife long to get her hands on it.

Though he often said that he ate too much, Vincent's asceticism was formidable. Like St. Dominic he never slept in bed, always on the floor, and he never sat to read or write; he always stood or knelt. He firmly believed that most people wore too many clothes. "If you feel cold, take something off—you'll feel warm when you put it on again," he advised. Like some Tibetan monks, and like some of the saints, he seemed able to generate his own heat.

At times his humor was worthy of Oscar Wilde: hearing nuns' confessions was, he said "like being nibbled to death by ducks." Yet throughout his life he retained a childlike simplicity and once tried to persuade a little girl visitor to preach to him from the pulpit at Haverstock Hill. When she proved too shy to attempt a sermon, Vincent was genuinely disappointed. "I'm sure I should have learned much from you, dear child," he said as he helped her down. And he meant it.

A colleague, passing his door late one night, heard him say: "Now, dear Lord, please go away. Brother Vincent wants to sleep."

He was businesslike, though, in his approach to death; ever considerate of others, he worked hard at winding up his affairs. "I've found that dying is a full-time job," he told his Hyde Park audience with a smile.

Those who heard his final lecture have an unforgettable memory of his parting message: "Jesus Christ is Love, Love, Love." His voice was very faint now, yet strangely, it could be heard even at the edge of the large crowd.

Vincent McNabb, O.P., died on June 17, 1943. "I *am* sorry—he wasn't such a bad old stick," said one of his fiercest hecklers.

Ten years later, from that same platform on which he had so often spoken, one of his Dominican confrères asked Catholics in the Hyde Park audience to sign a petition for the opening of his Cause.

IX

Towards the East

As soon as the two officials announced their business, the Prioress knew that something sinister was afoot.

"We have come to supervise the voting by the nuns," they announced.

"That will not be necessary," the Prioress told them. "Although ours is an enclosed order, the Sisters are always allowed out to vote in the normal way."

One of the men, evidently the senior, snapped back: "The polling will take place here in the convent—immediately."

Long years of Carmelite training helped the Prioress to retain her calm. It was useless to argue with these men, she knew that. They were Nazis and they had their orders.

When each nun had recorded her vote, the senior official consulted a list.

"Two persons have not voted," he declared. "Anna Fitzeck is missing."

"She does not have a vote—she is mentally handicapped," the Prioress explained.

The junior man made a note. The Prioress knew only too well what was coming next.

"And Dr. Edith Stein? Where is she?"

The Prioress strove even harder not to betray her anxiety. "Sister Mary Benedicta is not entitled to vote."

"Why not?"

"She is not Aryan."

Both men stared at her for a moment. When the senior spoke, his voice was hard.

"Write that down," he ordered. "Dr. Edith Stein, otherwise known as Sister Mary Benedicta—Non-Aryan."

With that, the two men departed. In the election, to nobody's surprise, the Nazis won a landslide victory.

She could no longer stay in the Cologne Carmel—Edith realised that at once. The presence of a Jewish nun in any German convent would soon bring harassment, and perhaps worse, on the whole community.

But Holland was safe, for this was still 1938, and the Carmel at Echt offered her a loving welcome. So to Echt she went, driven by a kindly doctor friend.

As they neared the Dutch border, he stopped at a wayside shrine of Our Lady of Peace. There Edith knelt and prayed for Germany, the country of her birth; the country which, though she did not know it then, she was leaving for the last time.

It had been a long, winding road which had brought her from a devoutly orthodox home, via years of atheism, at last to the Catholic Church and to Carmel. Perhaps she looked back over it, this beautiful, dark-eyed woman of forty-seven, as the car sped through the flat Dutch countryside.

Edith was born in Breslau on October 12th, 1891. Her father, a timber merchant, died when she was a baby, and upon Frau Stein fell the double responsibility of running the business and caring for a growing family of seven. Fortunately she was a tough, energetic woman—qualities which her youngest child inherited to the full.

One of her brothers, Paul, had a great love of literature and he would often talk to Edith about Goethe, Schiller and Heine as he carried her around in his arms. By the time she was four, little Jitschel—as her family called her—could reel off salient details about all the major German poets.

There was friction when she went to kindergarten—no place for a four-year-old intellectual. Having swiftly exhausted the teacher, Edith was returned home to await her sixth birthday, when she could go to a proper school and do proper lessons.

It was during her later schooldays that she got her first taste of antisemitism, when she was passed over for a prize which everyone knew that she had won. Ironically, she had by this time already abandoned her Jewish faith, at least inwardly. She went to synagogue still, but only to please her mother. At thirteen, Edith no longer believed in God.

Though a Jewess born, Edith admired the Prussian character; throughout her own life she practised its iron self-discipline. At school she was invariably top of the class. Yet she did not suffer the unpopularity which often goes with that position, for she had a warm and affectionate nature beneath her outer reserve, and her flashes of humor were all the more delightful for being unexpected. Furthermore she was not *quite* perfect; in arithmetic lessons her brilliance sometimes failed to shine, and when that happened she was not above copying the answers from her friend Katharina.

Edith did not study to beat her classmates and win prizes, but because she loved knowledge for its own sake. In one of her school essays she wrote: "A translator must be like a pane of glass, letting all the light through while itself remaining invisible."

The teenager had produced an epigram worthy of a classical author, and although she did not do that every day, she had a maturity of judgement far beyond her years. Small wonder that when she left, the headmaster made a pun on her surname: "Strike the stone (*stein*) and wisdom will spring forth."

At the University of Breslau she enrolled as a student of German language and literature, but philosophy was a compulsory subject and soon she realised that here was where her heart lay. In particular, she was captivated by the new school of thought known as phenomenology, whose leading exponent, Edmund Husserl, was then teaching at the University of Gottingen.

So hooked on Husserl was she that her friends twitted her about it. At a New Year party they made up a song which contained the following immortal lines:

> Other maidens dream of kisses;
> Husserl is what Edith wishes.

(In German the philosopher's name is made to rhyme with *busserl,* an Austrian dialect-word for "kisses").

After two years at Breslau, Edith's dream came true. With a girl friend she moved to Göttingen to study under the great man.

Though she would have been astonished had anyone told her so, Edith had in fact taken a step towards her eventual conversion to the Catholic Church. Phenomenology asserted that there was a real and objective world which could be known by the human mind: a view much more in tune with traditional Catholic philosophy than the prevailing idealism.

Husserl had himself joked that he ought to be canonised, since so many of his pupils became Catholics (though born a Jew, he was now a Lutheran). We can only guess at what he might have said could he have known that one of those pupils would become, not only a Catholic, but eventually a candidate for sainthood.

Before meeting her idol, Edith had to present herself to his assistant, Max Reinach. Soon she was a firm friend of this kindly young philosopher and the pretty wife whom he had recently married.

At her first, awestruck encounter with Husserl, Edith told him that she had read the whole of his masterwork *Logical Investigations,* including the difficult second volume. "You have?" smiled Husserl, eyes twinkling. "That really is heroic."

Among the students at his seminars, Edith's razor-sharp mind soon showed its quality. So it was not really surprising that in 1916, when he became Professor of Philosophy at Freiburg, Husserl invited her to go with him as his assistant.

A short time before, such an offer would have been beyond

her wildest hopes. She ought to have been happy—but some-how she was not. She had now spent years in the study of philosophy. She was at the right hand of the teacher she ad-mired above all. And yet . . . her quest for truth remained unsatisfied.

As she worked on Husserl's papers, producing order from mountains of rough shorthand notes, the conviction grew within her that neither phenomenology nor any other philo-sophical system could answer her ultimate need. Could reli-gion help her? She could never return to the Jewish faith of her childhood; of that she was sure. But what of Christianity?

During her first year at university she had been required to study the Lord's Prayer in the old High German language and this careful, word-by-word analysis had made a deep impres-sion on her. Now she began to ponder upon the prayer once again.

Among Husserl's Catholic converts was Max Scheler, a Jew like herself; a brilliant but erratic character who twice aban-doned his Catholic faith, the second time never to return to it. When Edith knew him he was between apostasies and at his most fervent. Whatever his faults, he helped her on the journey which she had now begun.

In 1917 Adolf Reinach was killed while fighting for Ger-many. He too had been a Jew, but both he and his wife had, like Husserl, been baptised as Lutherans. Edith, herself grief-stricken, went to see the young widow, dreading that she would find her distraught.

To her surprise, Anna Reinach was completely calm: her Christian faith had given her courage to bear her loss. At this time she was still a Protestant, though subsequently she was received into the Catholic Church.

Of her visit to Anna, Edith wrote later: "It was then that I first came face to face with the Cross and the divine strength which it gives to those who bear it . . . Christ streamed out upon me."

Even so, Edith did not become a Christian, not yet. It was not in her nature to rush into things.

In 1921 she spent a holiday with friends who ran a farm at Berzgabern. Among their books she found St. Teresa of Avila's autobiography. Quite literally she could not put it down—and she did not, until she had finished the last page. When she did finally close it, in the small hours of the morning, she knew that she must become a Catholic.

Baptised on New Year's Day, 1922, she travelled home to Breslau to break the news. For the first time in her life, she saw her mother cry.

To comfort her, Edith went several times with her to the synagogue. To Frau Stein's great astonishment, her daughter followed the service closely, reading the psalms from a Catholic breviary which she had brought along. In this way, Edith tried to show her mother that her baptism was no act of treachery—that indeed she had rediscovered the faith of her childhood in all its glorious fulfilment.

Almost as soon as she knew she must enter the Church, Edith knew that she must also follow St. Teresa by becoming a Carmelite nun. Yet she could not bring herself to enter at once. Her mother, already shattered by her conversion, might not survive the loss of her daughter behind convent walls.

The next eight years she spent teaching at a girls' school run by the Dominican nuns at Speyer, a medieval city beside the Rhine. There she spent long hours in prayer, reciting the Divine Office each day. She was asked to teach Latin to the younger Sisters; soon she was giving spiritual conferences as well. Although Edith was a laywoman and a recent convert, the nuns had realised that here was a very exceptional person indeed.

She was, inevitably, a strict and demanding teacher. When a girl said that she could not write an essay because she had injured her right hand, Edith told her to do it with her left. On another occasion the same pupil turned in an essay so stuffed with quotations that it seemed like a currant bun. She expected a good mark, but it came back inscribed: "The use of quotations proves that *other* people are clever."

Yet her door was always open to anyone with a problem and

she proved the wisest of counsellors to nuns and schoolgirls alike. She was never flippant or sarcastic, but she knew how to laugh. German schoolteachers of the nineteen-twenties often thought it their duty to be formidable. Edith's pupils, meeting her outside the classroom, were first surprised and then delighted at her easy, friendly manner.

When the girls studied *Hamlet* in school, Edith won permission for them to see the play performed in the professional theater—an unheard-of concession. Throughout her life she was an ardent campaigner for women's education; even as a Carmelite, she did not hide her opinion that the Church had much still to do in this area. She considered herself a feminist, though not everyone would call her so today, for she always insisted on women's helping, serving role as being essential to her nature.

During her eight years at Speyer, Edith worked at nights on German translations of Newman and Thomas Aquinas. She kept abreast of philosophical thought and she grew in her love of prayer. But there was another side to her life. Often she could be seen slipping quietly into town with a parcel under her arm—a present for some poor family or for someone down on his luck.

Despite her warm and affectionate personality, Edith seems never to have enjoyed any romantic attachments, either before or after she became a Catholic. "Academic life imposes its own obligations," she confided in later years. "I have always lived like a nun."

She finally entered Carmel in 1934, after a period as a college lecturer in Munster. As she had feared, her mother took the parting very badly, though she bravely tried not to blame Christ for taking away her daughter. "I won't say anything against Him," she cried in her distress. "He may have been a very good man. But why did he make himself God?"

Frau Stein was now eighty-four years old and to leave her almost tore Edith's heart out. Yet even as she said good-bye she knew even more certainly that she was doing what was right.

"Is she a good needlewoman?" one of the Cologne nuns asked anxiously, when she learned that Dr. Edith Stein was to enter as a postulant. In the convent, for the first time in her life, the philosopher found herself working hard with mop and duster, and it has to be said that she did not do very well at it. Nevertheless she was a trier, even the most exacting of her Sisters had to admit that as they watched her rubbing her way gamely along the corridors.

Before she entered the convent, Edith had sometimes been guilty of looking askance at those who did not come up to her own high standards of duty and self-discipline. In particular, she could not understand how anyone could grow tired while at prayer. One day, soon after entering the convent, she said as much.

The other nuns were living the Carmelite rule in all its strictness and they understood very well how tiring it could be. However, they made no comment, they just waited. Came the day when Edith, now herself following the Rule, fell asleep at her prayers. She was never censurious again.

As she grew into her new life, she became more relaxed, more gay. St. Teresa of Avila, that most cheerful of saints, had laughed loud and often, and now Edith did the same, sometimes until the tears ran down her cheeks.

Her superiors did not wish her talents to lie buried. They encouraged her to write. She produced a study of Husserl's philosophy in relation to that of St. Thomas, and much other work besides.

Yet over these happy, fruitful years lay the shadow of the swastika—a shadow that for her became a reality when the two Nazi officials knocked at the door of the Cologne Carmel on that election day in 1938.

When she fled to Holland it was for the sake of her Sisters. It was not in her nature to seek safety for herself, nor did she desire it.

Edith, who had been born on the Jewish Day of Atonement, now offered her own life as a sacrifice for peace, praying that a new world war might be avoided. She wrote out her wish in a note to her new Prioress in the Carmel at Echt. The note, still preserved, is dated March 26th, 1939—Passion Sunday.

When war broke out and the Nazis invaded Holland, her sacrifice was accepted. Her superiors had arranged that she should go to a Carmel in Switzerland, together with her sister Rosa, who had been baptised and who had come to live near the convent at Echt. As the formalities for her exit visa were being completed, the Dutch bishops published a pastoral letter protesting at the Nazis' ill-treatment of the Jews. The Nazis retaliated swiftly. Among their victims were Edith and Rosa Stein.

Arrested and taken to a camp at Westerbork, they were roughly treated by the S.S. and thrust into a hut where they spent the day without food. Among their fellow prisoners were young mothers with babies. Many of these poor women were too dazed and frightened to look after their children properly. A Jew who escaped told later of a Carmelite nun who moved serenely from group to group, comforting the mothers and tending the little ones.

The last person to see Edith alive was one of her old pupils from the Dominican school at Speyer. As she stood on the station platform at Schifferstadt, she heard someone calling to her by her maiden name, and saw Edith at the window of a train crammed with Jewish prisoners. "Give my love to the Sisters at St. Magdalena," she said. "I am going towards the East."

Two days later, on August 9, 1942, Edith Stein and her sister died in the gas-chamber at Auschwitz.

X

With Christ in Dachau

Swiftly and efficiently, the nurse filled her syringe and reached for her patient's arm. Outwardly she was calm: she had done this job many times before and she would do it many times more. Yet she knew, even as she pressed the syringe home, that this time was different.

As the lethal fluid entered his body, the man looked at her steadily. Many others had died on the straw mattress where he lay, some of them filled with fear and hatred. Yet he was calm—far calmer than she herself was. His face showed neither fear nor hatred, but something infinitely more disturbing: compassion and love. Ten minutes later, he was dead.

As his body was carted off to the crematorium, the nurse looked at the rosary—his own rosary—which he had given to her a few days before. She had not wanted to take it, had told him that she could no longer pray.

"At least you can say the second part, 'pray for us sinners,'" he had replied. So she kept it.

Meanwhile, the whisper ran through the concentration camp: "Titus is dead." Prisoners in Dachau quickly learned to treat death with a shrug of the shoulders, yet this news brought profound sadness. For the frail Dutch priest, sick before ever he arrived, had brought joy and hope to everyone around him. It was for him that even the guards kept their cruellest treatment.

Titus Brandsma died at 2 p.m. on Sunday, July 26th, 1942. We know the exact time and date because the Nazis, meticulous as always, issued a neatly-typed death certificate. The name on the document is not Titus—the name he took when he entered the Calced Carmelites—but Anno, his baptismal name.

Anno Brandsma was born on February 23rd, 1881, at Oegeklooster in the province of Friesland, in the extreme North of Holland. Frisians are mainly dour Calvinist farmers with, it is said, the law of predestination written in their faces.

The Brandsmas were farmers and they were dour, but they were staunch Catholics. Three of Anno's four sisters became nuns and his only brother became a Franciscan priest. Anno, like his brother, attended a Franciscan school but decided not to join that order because of fears that he might not be strong enough for the tough pastoral life—an ironic decision in view of the whirlwind energy which later marked his career as a Carmelite.

At the age of twenty, while still a student, Anno—now Brother Titus—published an anthology drawn from the writings of St. Teresa of Avila, and he soon made a name for himself as a lively-minded fellow who plagued his rigidly conservative theology professor with questions which were then considered daring. He also ran a highly-successful magazine which argued, among other things, that too much apostolic talent was buried behind monastery walls and that today's contemplatives should—like their medieval predecessors—play their part in shaping the modern world.

We must not think that, because he held these views, Titus was a restless contemplative. No one sang the Divine Office with more vigor than he. Indeed, in choir he made such a joyful noise unto the Lord that his brethren sometimes had to ask him to tone it down a little. Now and throughout his life he seemed to get from the Office the energy which he needed for his dynamic activity.

Looking back on his student years, Titus saw himself somewhat ruefully as a stubborn young man with pronounced—often too pronounced—views of his own. "I was very conceited," he recalls, though his friends thought that judgement too harsh. Certainly he was never afraid to express an opinion. However, he endeared himself to everyone, even those who disagreed with him, by his natural cheerfulness and his readiness to help anyone who needed him. His photos at this time show an alert, studious young man with spectacles, a shock of brown hair, and a wide mouth that always seems about to break into a grin.

Of his intellectual brilliance there could be no doubt. Even at school, a master had told him jokingly: "You are too clever to be a Franciscan. You had better become a Jesuit!" After his ordination therefore, his Carmelite superiors might have been expected to give him an academic post.

But the dogmatic theology professor, whose word carried much weight, argued against it. Titus was unreliable, he declared. His advanced views might do harm and embarrass the order. So Titus was appointed a sacristan and financial administrator.

Now it so happened that this same professor, Dr. Eugenius Driessen, had a brother, also a Carmelite, who was even more influential than himself. Dr. Hubertus Driessen was serving in Rome as Procurator of the entire order, and when he heard what had been decided he moved swiftly. Saved at the eleventh hour from candlewax and balance-sheets, Titus was borne off to Rome by his rescuer to study at the Gregorian University.

While a philosophy student in Holland, Titus had suffered a severe haemorrhage and been confined to bed for several weeks. In Rome he suffered another, this one so bad that for a time his life was in danger. However he recovered and, at the age of twenty-eight, he received his doctorate.

For the next fourteen years, Titus taught Carmelite students in the seminary at Oss. Once again he launched a paper, which soon had a circulation of 11,000 copies. Its aim—and it succeeded mightily—was to make the work of the Carmelites known throughout Holland.

As you will have gathered, his interest in journalism was more than amateur. His great ambition was to launch a national daily with an editorial policy based on Catholic social teaching. In Rome, he had studied sociology with this in view. He never saw this plan realised, but his enthusiasm remained undimned. Many of his friends were journalists and he often impressed them with his deep technical knowledge of their craft. In fact, for a time he actually edited the local weekly paper at Oss. It was this lifelong interest in pressmen and the press that was to lead to his death in Dachau.

Had Titus gone into business, he would almost certainly have made his first million before he was thirty. As it was, he became a spiritual tycoon, generating ideas and firing everyone around him with his own special kind of enthusiasm.

As though teaching and journalism were not enough, he embarked with three other Carmelites on a great work of scholarship: a translation of all St. Teresa of Avila's works into Dutch. He saw three of the seven volumes off the press; the remaining four he never saw, for they were not published until after the war.

During these years, also, he led an energetic campaign to have Frisian—his own native tongue—recognised as an official language of the Netherlands. Frisian is not a dialect but a language in its own right, as different from Dutch as Welsh is from English. Thanks to the work of Titus and his friends, it is now an official language, fostered with Government money and taught in the schools.

Many of those friends were Protestants, and it gave Titus especial pleasure to work with them. As a young friar he had asked to be allowed to join the Apostolate for Reunion, and he remained an active member right up to the time of his arrest.

And he toured Holland raising money for the Carmelite missions in Brazil.

By this time you may be wondering how this super-friar found time to say any prayers. In fact, in addition to Mass and private prayer, he continued to sing the whole Divine Office each day along with his Carmelite brethren, and he was distressed when—after yet another serious illness—his superiors ordered him to rest instead of going to choir.

In 1923 he was appointed to teach philosophy at the Catholic University of Nijmegen. Now he was busier than ever, for philosophy was not his first love and he had to do much reading to prepare himself for his classes. Nevertheless he still found time for anyone who needed his help, or who just wanted to talk. A friend of that time has given us a vivid picture of Titus sitting at the typewriter in his room, hammering out his lecture notes and at the same time carrying on a conversation with a crowd of chattering students. Yet his lectures were always perfectly constructed and he had a total grasp of his material.

He did not merely devote himself to his students: all manner of men were his friends. He got jobs for people who were out of work, solicited commissions for struggling artists, cheered up people who were lonely or depressed, brought total strangers back to his room for coffee.

Though a profound student of mysticism—he became an authority on Ruysbroek and the mystical writers of the Low Countries—he was no stern ascetic. As he freely admitted, he loved what are commonly called the good things in life. Like many Dutchmen he was very fond of cigars, he also smoked a pipe—and he was always ready to try something new.

On his first visit to Ireland, he tasted Irish whiskey and found it splendid. Indeed, he liked it so much that he knocked back several glasses, somewhat to the alarm of his Carmelite host. Fortunately, the drink seemed to have no marked effect.

In 1932 he was appointed Rector Magnificus of the University, though anyone less "magnificus" than Titus it would be hard to imagine. A Roman Cardinal, confronted with the boyish-looking Dutchman, assumed that the Rector was ill and had sent a young deputy in his place.

Extrovert that he was, Titus said little directly about his own interior life, but his articles and lectures open a large window on to his soul. As one would expect of any Carmelite, he had a deep devotion to the Virgin Mary. Indeed, it was the order's special relationship with her that led him to Carmel in the first place. It is not surprising, therefore, to find Mary given a prominent place in his rectorial address:

"Just as Revelation leads us to acknowledge the child in her arms as God, so may she guide our minds to contemplate God in the whole of His creation. As He lived in her, may He live in us and, born of our deeds, make his entry into the world."

More than once he uttered this same idea: that we must imitate Our Lady by letting God be born, first in ourselves and then in the world around us. It follows, according to Titus, that mysticism is not just for mystics: everyone is called to this highest kind of union with God.

This proposition sounds startling even today, yet Titus hammered it home again and again, returning to the theme during a visit to the United States in 1935. "Of course, the mystical life is, and always remains, a gift of God." he added. "But God has made our nature susceptible to it."

His tour of the States took in New York, Chicago, Washington, Allentown, Middletown and Niagara Falls—where he underwent one of the mystical experiences of his own life.

"I see God in the work of his hands and the marks of his love in every visible thing," he wrote later, "and it sometimes happens that I am seized by a supreme joy which is above all other joys."

As always, however, Titus had both feet planted very firmly in this world. Before he set sail, the Archbishop of Utrecht had asked him to become spiritual adviser to Holland's Catholic journalists, and he used his American tour to gather valuable advice from teachers of journalism in U.S. universities.

When he got back home, he wanted to open a center for

training journalists at Nijmegen, but this, too, was a project that was to come to pass only after his death.

Inevitably Titus had his critics. Some colleagues thought his ideas too often grandiose and impractical. For them, he had this reply:

"Christ cannot live in us if we don't allow him a chance. We are so afraid of public opposition that we hold ourselves far too much in check. Then one looks in vain for charity, sacrifice and courage."

Sacrifice and courage . . . so far, Titus had shown plenty of both. Soon, he was to show the supreme sacrifice and the supreme courage.

First, however, he underwent yet another serious illness—not a haemorrhage this time but a disease of the spinal marrow which attacked the brain and affected both memory and concentration. For a man of his intellectual gifts it was a cruel blow, but he bore it with his usual cheerfulness. Two years later, in December, 1939, a severe urinary infection added to his troubles. Still he refused to become downcast.

"The bacilli are up-to-date and treacherous," he joked. "They attack without declaring war."

This wisecrack was, of course, a reference to the Nazis, who at that moment were spreading through Europe like a deadly plague. Four months later they invaded Holland.

During that terrible occupation, Titus went quietly and cheerfully about his work, refusing to be depressed or frightened. He interceded successfully to get a widow's son out of a German prison. To his brother Henry, the Franciscan, who was suffering badly from nerves, he wrote: "The Lord grant you joy above all. Try to live calmly and be relaxed. Put all your confidence in God, come what may, for He is always with us."

At that very moment Titus was himself a marked man, and he knew it.

From the outset, the Nazi occupation had presented the Catholic editors with serious moral problems. How far could they legitimately go in obeying the Germans? At what point must they dig their heels in and refuse?

At once they turned to Titus, their spiritual adviser. Where possible, he tried to find a formula which would satisfy the Catholic conscience without provoking a confrontation. But soon, they all knew, a confrontation must come.

At the end of 1941 the Germans demanded that the Catholic papers run Nazi propaganda advertisements. In a secret letter, which he delivered to each editor personally, Titus counselled that no paper could publish such propaganda and remain Catholic. The editors, naturally, were deeply worried, but Titus was convinced that the Nazis would not force the issue.

He was right: they did not. But they knew about the letter, knew its contents, knew who had encouraged the editors to stand against them. Someone had betrayed Titus.

"The Germans are after me. They say I am committing sabotage . . . But I am going to carry on." In these words, Titus made clear to his friends that he fully understood the danger which he was in. To those who wanted him to hide, he replied that it was unthinkable. How could he expect the journalists to stand firm if he, their adviser, ran away?

At 6 p.m. on January 19th, two members of the secret police arrived at the Nijmegen Carmel. "Pray for me," said Titus to his brethren, as they took him away.

"Now I am going to get a cell of my own. I am going to be a real Carmelite!" So Titus had joked when he knew that his arrest was near. The cell was at Scheveningen, near the Hague, in a prison which the Nazis had fashioned from a hotel. Here he spent nearly two months under interrogation. At Scheveningen he was not ill-treated; indeed his interrogator, Hardegen, treated him courteously and later paid him a grudging tribute. "He is a man of strong character," Hardegen declared, "but he is highly dangerous."

The interrogation was a battle between two razor-sharp intellects. Like St. Thomas More, Titus did not seek martyrdom; he used all his skill in argument in an effort to preserve his life if he could. But it soon became clear that the Nazis had no intention of releasing him: they knew his mettle only too well.

On March 12th he was taken to the concentration camp at Amersfoort, near Utrecht. Now his Calvary had begun. Dressed in prison clothes, his head shaven, Titus was forced, sich as he was, to work with pickaxe and spade in temperatures often below freezing.

When dysentery broke out among the prisoners, Titus, though himself a sufferer, nursed and comforted his fellows. Soon all of them had learned to love him; Protestants, Jews and unbelievers no less than Catholics. To call a priest "Father" was dangerous, so most of them simply used his first name. To the young he was "Uncle" Titus—a title which younger Dutch people frequently give to elders of whom they are fond.

All his life he had sought and prayed for unity with non-Catholic Christians: now it became a living reality. Frequently he joined in prayer with the Protestant ministers who were suffering with him. One of them said later that to pray with Titus was truly a foretaste of that union which Jesus desired—and still desires—for us all.

Yet around them lay hatred, more palpable than guns or barbed wire: the hatred of their captors for Christianity in general and Catholicism in particular. Prisoners were not allowed even to mention the name of Christ, and ministers of religion—Protestant and Catholic alike—were often subjected to half an hour of gruelling physical exercise when they were already exhausted from their day's work. Titus was not spared even this ordeal.

On Good Friday, 1942, the camp at Dachau—to which he was shortly to go—saw a terrible parody of the Church's liturgy for the day. A priest was crowned with thorns, a Jew was forced to read the Passion, and other priests were forced to sing the hymn *O Haupt voll Blut und Wunden,* ('O Sacred Head Ill-Used').

Titus, at that very moment was giving a talk to his fellow prisoners at Amersfoort. Ostensibly it was on the history of mysticism—a subject designed to evade the Nazi ban on religious topics. In fact, it became a profound meditation on the sufferings of Christ—a discourse which had a lifelong effect on everyone who heard it.

The Nazis could not fail to be aware of what he had done. Plainly Titus Brandsma was a dangerous man, even in a concentration camp. His fate was sealed.

He was moved back briefly to Scheveningen, where he attracted the hostility of a coarse, brutal guard named Kirzig, who enjoyed using obscenities in his presence. Slowly, however, Titus's kindly and serene manner began to have an unforeseen effect. Kirzig was not immediately won over, but his curiosity was roused. One evening he took Titus along to his guard-room and kept him talking there far into the night. Long afterwards, he told a colleague: "That man was a saint."

In the earliest days of the Church, Christian prisoners were frequently offered their freedom if they would offer a pinch of incense to the Roman gods. During his second stay at Scheveningen, it is believed, a similar offer was made by Titus. He could go free if he would make a small retraction of his anti-Nazi views. He refused.

He arrived in Dachau, after a long and terrible journey, on June 19th, 1942. Among his companions was a young Protestant minister named Kapteyn. At Amersfoort the two men had become close friends. Now Kapteyn, like Titus, was soon to die.

Titus's chief tormentor was a guard named Walther Thiele, a man of exceptional brutality even by Nazi standards. When Titus had difficulty in making his bed in the regulation manner, Thiele beat him up in front of the other prisoners, kicking him again and again as he lay helpless on the ground.

Later in the day, Thiele would find fault with the way in which Titus had washed his eating dish, and another beating would follow. Once Thiele was seen knocking Titus in the face with the dish until he bled freely. On another occasion, Titus was beaten and kicked while carrying the Blessed Sacrament—for Mass was said in the cell-blocks where German priests were held, and they used to smuggle consecrated hosts to their non-German brethern.

As Thiele strode away, Titus got up slowly and managed a grin. "I was not worried because I knew Whom I had with me," he said.

Despite this ill-treatment, Titus prayed constantly for the Nazi guards and sometimes tried to talk to them, to bring them back to sanity. Friends, afraid that this would only bring more beatings, tried to dissuade him. "Perhaps something will stick—who knows?" Titus replied gently.

On the day after that last cruel beating, a senior guard named Becker came to the window of Block 28 and looked Titus up and down. "You look pretty ill, Brandsma," he said, not unkindly. "You had better go into the hospital."

It was not the first time the offer had been made. Now, Titus was too weak to refuse.

The hospital, he knew, was no oasis of mercy, but a place where Nazi doctors practised cruel and degrading experiments on their defenseless patients. Once again Titus was not spared. As he suffered, he said aloud: "Not my will but Thine be done."

What we know about his last hours we owe to the nurse who gave him the last fatal injection. Like Titus she was Dutch, and he was deeply disturbed when he found that she was a lapsed Catholic.

"I shall pray for you much," he said as he gave her his rosary. And he did.

Later the nurse returned to the practise of her faith. She has given her own account of Titus's death to the authorities investigating his Cause.

Never once during all his sufferings does Titus seem to have felt even a moment of despair. When others were at their lowest, he consoled them in words that live for us all:

"We are here in a dark tunnel. We must pass through it. Somewhere at the end shines the eternal light."

XI

Bakhita, the Lucky Slave

The girls were startled when the Arabs appeared suddenly from the barley-field. Why were these men, both strangers, lurking there among the tall grain?

The older of the two smiled smoothly.

"Do not be afraid, little ones," he said. "We are only two poor travellers. We have come far across the Sudan—and we still have a great way to go."

So gracious was his manner that fear left them at once. The younger girl, a nine-year-old, obeyed readily when the Arab asked her, as a great favor, to fetch the parcel which he had left under a nearby tree.

"It will save our legs," he explained.

Her companion, who was fifteen, should have been suspicious when the two men told her to wait further along the path until the younger girl returned. But she did not suspect anything. She did as she was told.

Meanwhile, the nine-year-old had reached the tree. There was no parcel. She turned, puzzled. Both Arabs were standing behind her, knives at the ready.

"Make a sound and you are dead!"

That they meant it she had no doubt. Her screams would

bring the men of the village running from the nearby fields, and they would make short work of the Arabs—if they caught them. But by that time, she herself would be a corpse. Better to keep quiet.

As they hurried her through the waving barley, a jumble of questions cascaded through her mind. How had the men managed to creep up on her so quietly, without her friend seeing them? Why had they taken only her? And what were they going to do with her?

With sickening clarity a memory came back to her, of a day half-forgotten when she had still been little more than a baby. Her mother had gone to the fields, leaving herself and her twin sister in the care of an older sister who was married. Suddenly there had been a terrible commotion, with the men shouting and running everywhere, the women crying, and her mother screaming out her despair across the village.

When they were told what had happened, the two little girls did not really understand, but they cried anyway. Without anyone seeing them, Arabs like these had crept into the village and taken their married sister away. They had never seen her again.

How would her mother stand this second terrible blow, the child wondered, as the men finally stopped and faced her.

"Tell us, my dear, what is your name?"

The elder of the two, the one who had asked her to fetch the parcel, tried to smile reassuringly. He did not succeed. The little prisoner, half-paralyzed with fear, stared at her captor without replying.

"It doesn't matter," the man told her. "We'll give you a new name. From now on you will be called Bakhita. It's a nice name. It means the Lucky One."

But there's nothing lucky about me, thought Bakhita, as she lay in a locked hut with seven other captives. She knew now what her fate was to be. All of them were destined for the slave-market.

In the Sudan a century ago slavery was a thriving, highly-organised industry. Its victims, generally black like Bakhita herself, would often pass through the hands of two or three middle-men before finding a permanent owner.

After a night spent in the bare, windowless hut the victims were chained together and shepherded across the desert towards the rendezvous where a dealer would be waiting to strike a bargain with their captors. Three of the prisoners were men and three women. The seventh was a girl of Bakhita's own age.

As the sun rose in the sky, Bakhita thought once more of the parents she had left behind and of the home which she might never see again. She was unhappy and she was afraid, but her spirit was not broken. She resolved that if the chance came, she would escape.

Had her captors known what she was planning, they would have laughed. A mere child, and a negro child at that, run away into the unknown! No, Bakhita was born to be a slave—Allah had willed it—and a slave she would remain.

So they did not think they were risking anything when, during a pause in the journey, they took the chains from the two children and left them, unattended, to winnow some corn. In no time at all, the little girls were off into the forest.

They wandered for several miles, not knowing where they were heading, hoping that somehow they would find the road to home. What they found instead was a prowling lion.

Once again, there was no panic. From birth they had been taught exactly what to do in an emergency like this. Scrambling swiftly up the nearest tree, they remained there until the lion padded off to seek a dinner elsewhere.

Their next encounter was with a prowling Arab—and this time their luck was out. The children readily accepted his offer of a meal, only to find themselves, just as before, locked in a hut. Their escape had been in vain: in the morning they were sold to the agent of another slave-merchant and soon they were once again part of a chain-gang, plodding along to the slave-market of El Obeid.

This time they were closely guarded; there was no chance to break for freedom. When they reached El Obeid, the merchant himself took a fancy to Bakhita and gave her to his daughter. So the little peasant became a lady's maid.

It was not a bad life, as slavery went. With her gentle yet dignified disposition, and her sunny smile, she soon made herself popular and was treated well—for a while.

One day poor Bakhita had the ill-luck to break an ornamental vase belonging to the merchant's son, a spoiled, ill-tempered lout whose tantrums governed the household. Flying into a rage, he thrashed the child soundly and demanded that his father get rid of her.

In her next home she was miserable indeed. Her owner was a local Turkish officer, a henpecked man who might himself have been a slave for all the respect his womenfolk showed him. They seem to have been sadistically inclined and Bakhita was completely at their mercy: they flogged her regularly and tattooed her simply to gratify a fashionable whim. Sometimes she suffered even at the gentle officer's hands, for whenever his wife and daughters riled him he would take it out on his slaves.

Her luck changed again when her owner, travelling home to Turkey on leave, decided to sell off the slaves in Khartoum. Bakhita was bought by the Italian vice-consul, who treated her as a daughter while he tried to find out who her parents were so that he could send her back home. His efforts came to nothing—by this time Bakhita had even forgotten her original name. So he took her back with him to Italy.

At the hotel in Genoa, Bakhita and her guardian became friendly with a rich lady named Signora Michieli. The Signora's small daughter became so fond of the young Sudanese girl that the kindly vice-consul agreed to give her over to their care. So, at the age of fourteen, Bakhita found herself once more with a new owner.

The Michieli family owned a hotel at Suakim, on the Red Sea, and the plan was that Bakhita should eventually become a waitress there. She actually spent several months at the hotel with her mistress, but for the next six years she lived mainly at the family home near Venice, acting as companion to the little girl.

Just as she was about to move back to Suakim, the family steward stepped in with an unexpected request. Bakhita, nominally a Moslem, had received no instruction in the Christian faith. Should she not, he asked, remain in Italy long enough to learn something about it and then, if she wished, receive Baptism?

Signor Michieli was a lapsed Catholic and his wife Greek Orthodox. Nevertheless, they agreed that Bakhita's departure should be delayed. As the Signora prepared to travel without her, the young daughter, Mimmina, announced that she could not bear to be separated from her beloved companion even for a few months. So she, too, stayed behind and arrangements were made for both girls to board at the Venice convent of the Daughters of Charity of Canossa.

Centuries before Bakhita's time, before Islam swept through the Middle East, much of the Sudan had been Christian; early travellers spoke wonderingly of its churches and monasteries. Bakhita's people, the Daju, ruled over a stretch of territory in Darfur, where black Africa meets the Arab world. Her ancestors, therefore, may have been Christian—but Bakhita knew nothing of that. She only knew, when she entered the convent, that at last she had come home.

When Signora Michieli arrived back ten months later to claim the girl whom she still regarded as her property, she got an unpleasant shock. Nothing short of physical force, Bakhita declared, would ever make her leave the Canossian Sisters.

The illiterate slave-girl, pushed around all her life, now showed a dignity and strength of purpose which amazed everybody round her. All the pride and breeding of her ancient race had at last asserted itself—but there was more to her new-found determination than that. At the convent, Bakhita had learned well. If Christ's teaching were true, she demanded, how could anyone claim to own her body and soul?

The Mother Superior, who at first had sided with Signora

Michieli, began to have serious misgivings. Might not Bakhita, after all, be right? Signora Michieli was a good woman, certainly; but could she really lay claim to Bakhita as her slave?

Clearly this was a case for higher authority, for the Cardinal Patriarch himself. Since civil law was also involved, the Patriarch called in the King's Procurator. Two days later these high representatives of Church and State held court in the convent parlor to decide Bakhita's fate.

The hearing was heated, with Signora Michieli and her friends loudly demanding that the wayward slave-girl should return.

When Bakhita was invited to speak, she was brief—yet no lawyer could have bettered her argument.

"I love the Signora dearly," she said, "and to part from Mimmina cuts me to the heart. But I shall not leave this place because I cannot risk losing God."

Cardinal Agostini had no doubts about Bakhita's case, but the final verdict rested with the Procurator. He did not have any doubts either. Since slavery was illegal under Italian law, he ruled any slave was emancipated immediately he or she touched Italian soil. Bakhita was a free woman and no one would be permitted to interfere with her rights.

Mimmina was heart-broken, her mother furious. "Give that ungrateful girl a kiss, then forget her," she commanded. "You will never see her again."

On January 9, 1890, the former slave-girl was baptised by the Cardinal Patriarch, with a countess for her godmother and a great crowd of well-wishers all eager to welcome her into the Church. They gasped when she appeared, radiant in her purple dress and black veil—the veil being exchanged for a white one as soon as the water had been poured on her forehead.

It was not the affection of these people, or of the nuns who looked after her, that Bakhita found most wonderful. To the end of her days, she never ceased to marvel at God's love for her. Could it really be true, she had asked again and again, that in God's eyes she was someone who mattered, someone He cared for at every moment of her life? Sometimes she would hurry to the nearest available Sister just to be reassured once more.

In the end she was convinced. She, Bakhita, *was* somebody important; as important as Signora Michieli, as important as the Cardinal Patriarch—even as important as the Mother Superior. And so she became a Christian, with three new names. Josephine Margaret Fortunata. The last one was not, of course, really new; it was simply the Italian version of the name her Arab captors had given her, oh, so long ago it seemed now. Fortunata—the lucky one.

From the beginning she wanted to join the Canossian Order, but it took quite a while for her to pluck up sufficient courage to ask the Sisters to accept her as a postulant. A black Christian might be all very fine. But who ever heard of a black nun?

The question was a reasonable one: in the Europe of those days black religious were few indeed. When she did eventually confide her wish, she was swiftly assured that black nuns were just as acceptable as white ones. The Mother Superior, though delighted by her request, was not at all surprised. She had realised from the beginning that Bakhita had a vocation, but had refrained from approaching her because she did not wish to influence her in any way. The decision to enter had to be entirely her own.

So Bakhita became a Canossian Sister and remained one for more than fifty years, totally happy in whatever job she was given, with a kind word and a willing smile for everyone.

"Don't you have any passions like the rest of us?" asked one Sister, amazed at her cheerful equanimity.

"Of course I have," replied Bakhita with that familiar grin. "But when they trouble me I just say, 'Go away now and I'll attend to you later.'"

The terrible traumas of her childhood had left no mark on her personality, a fact which might well have surprised a psychiatrist. Her secret was, undoubtedly, that ever-present sense of God's love.

"If I had known it when I was a slave," she said, "I would never have suffered so much."

She wanted very much to return to the Sudan, to find her family and if possible, to help in the conversion of her fellow-countrymen.

"They are really good out there," she declared often. "They would make such fervent Christians."

Her wish was never granted. Instead her Superiors had her travel the length and breadth of Italy, rallying support for the missions at meetings where her audiences often included bishops and other dignitaries.

"Be good! Love God! Pray for the pagans!" She always ended her talks with these words, and they must have struck home to many.

In some towns there were traffic jams because of the crowds who turned out to hear her. They would have been surprised, looking at that always-smiling face, to know how the famous Mother Josephine really felt about her lecture-tours.

"No doubt everyone thought I was enjoying myself," she said years later, "but for me they were a slow martyrdom."

Yet she went on giving of her best, because that was what obedience demanded, and because she knew that she was helping the peoples of Africa who were always so close to her hearts.

For most of her long life Bakhita enjoyed excellent health, but in the last four years she suffered a barrage of ailments which slowly reduced her to absolute helplessness and cruelly disfigured her once-attractive face. Her mind, however, remained unimpaired—and so did her radiant personality.

Her greatest suffering was the trouble she caused to others, though none of her Sisters begrudged the care they gave to her. When they scolded her for not calling when she needed help, she replied with a smile: "Since I can no longer keep the Rule myself, the least I can do is let the rest of you keep it."

Sisters who came to her room to comfort "poor" Mother Josephine soon found their own spirits being lifted by the ever-cheerful patient. Brushing aside all talk of her own ailments, she demanded news of everything and everyone. When she did mention her illness, it was usually to joke about it.

"I'm all skin and bone—there'll be nothing left for the worms!" she said, as disease wasted her away.

She died on February 8th, 1947, at Schio, close to the Italian Alps. She had lived for many years in the convent there and the townsfolk regarded her as their own. Her funeral was more a triumphal procession than a solemn farewell, and the splendid marble monument later erected over her grave, with its florid recital of her virtues, would certainly have made her chuckle.

No more colorful story appears in these pages than hers, and yet we should not let that blind us to her true importance. If Bakhita is eventually canonized, it will not be because her early life was dramatic, but rather because of the merit which she gained during the long, undramatic years which followed.

XII

Doctor America

There was a good deal of banter as Tom Dooley climbed on to the operating table to have the lump on his chest removed. To his assistants it seemed funny to see the great Dr. Dooley suddenly reduced to the rank of patient in his own hospital at Mvong Sing in Laos.

It was only a very minor operation, performed under a local anesthetic. Jokes seemed to be in order. The young American himself managed a wisecrack or two as his older colleague, Dr. William Van Vallin, skilfully went to work.

It was Bill Van Vallin, on a visit from the States, who had suggested that the lump should come off. It had been giving Tom a good deal of pain and both men thought that it was a sebaceous cyst. Only when the operation was finished did Tom see the "cyst" for himself.

"Bill—it's jet black."

Tom spoke with some surprise. Dr. Van Vallin kept his professional calm.

"Yes, Tom," he replied. "It is."

The tumor was placed in formalin to be analysed at a well-equipped hospital in Bangkok. Dr. Van Vallin left with it, and Tom Dooley went back to work. The lump, he now decided, was not a cyst after all, but almost certainly a calcified blood clot from a fall which he had suffered some time before.

In fact it was a malignant melanoma—a deadly form of cancer. Eighteen months later, on the day after his 34th birthday, Tom Dooley died in New York. Thousands filed past his coffin. A TV newscaster, attempting to cover the scene, broke down and wept.

"He had so little time, but how superbly he used it." The *New York Times* spoke for all the millions who admired him. At an age when most clever young doctors are only beginning to make their mark, Tom was internationally famous. People all over the world knew of his work for the stricken people of Southeast Asia. Medico, the organisation he founded, brought medical aid to thousands who would otherwise have died without hope.

While he was alive, Tom had his critics. He was accused of arrogance, impatience, exhibitionism. There were those who said that fame had gone to his head. Others rejected these charges indignantly. Those who made them, they declared, did not know the real Tom Dooley.

Certainly Tom had no illusions about himself. He insisted that would-be recruits to Medico be warned in advance that Dooley was a difficult fellow to work for. One of his best friends told him: "If you are a saint, then you wear your halo at a mighty crooked angle." Needless to say, Tom never made any such claim—he would have laughed at the very idea. Yet today many who knew him are convinced that a saint is exactly what he was. Already the first stage in his Cause has begun.

Thomas Anthony Dooley III was born in St. Louis, Missouri, on January 17th, 1927. His father, an engineer, was an executive of the American Car and Foundry Company. His mother, daughter of a Pennsylvania family, had been married previously to an Air Force pilot who was killed soon after World War I. The growing family divided their time between the spacious home in St. Louis and their six-bedroomed "cottage" at Green Lake, Wisconsin.

Tom's earliest talent was for music: he could read notes before he could read words and at four he was already playing simple pieces on the piano. At grade school he showed a flare for languages which stood him in good stead when he went to Asia. But French was always the language that he loved most. Aided by summer courses at the Sorbonne, he became fluent in it.

Tom Dooley was a clever young fellow, no doubt about that. He was good-looking, too, and he had plenty of charm. He drew girls like a magnet and could jitterbug formidably, flipping his partner over his back in a fashion rarely seen outside Hollywood. He was a dashing horseman.

It was his boundless energy and self-confidence that really made people notice him. He was overawed by no one. Once, when he was still a schoolboy, his mother worried in case his enthusiastic collecting for charity might offend neighbors, some of them eminent people. "Why, Mother," replied Tom indignantly, "they're really the same as everyone else, aren't they?"

When Tom announced that he wanted to be a doctor, his father opposed the idea. Tom, he feared, might have too much drive and too little patience to survive the years of grinding study. He also thought his son too artistic to be a medical man.

In the end Tom got his way, but first came a stint as a medical corpsman in the Navy, where he distinguished himself by persuading Hildegarde, a night-club singer of renown, to visit his patients in the Navy Hospital at St. Albans, Long Island. The lady refused to be escorted on her tour of the hospital by anyone but Corpsman Dooley. And escorted she was, with the bemused "brass" trailing along behind.

He loved the Navy so much that he decided to return to it once his studies at Notre Dame were complete. During his student years, Tom's superabundant energy and his impatience with the routine of classes and clinics sometimes brought him into collision with authority. However he safely graduated from medical school in March, 1953 and the following month began his internship in the Naval Hospital at Camp Pendleton, California.

Postings to Japan and the Philippines followed. Then, late in 1954, Tom was ordered to Vietnam to help in the transfer of the half-million refugees who chose exile in the South rather than life under the Communists in the North.

From his arrival in Japan Tom had been fascinated with the Orient: its language, its religions, its culture. Many of its values appealed to him deeply—especially the reverence for old age and the care which older children took of younger. It hurt him when his patients, because he was an American, treated him with fear and suspicion. And yet he understood well enough why they felt that way. Experience had taught them to equate a while skin with colonialism and exploitation.

Soon many had been won over by Tom's happy, forceful personality and by his medical skill. Like the Pied Piper he could charm a boatload of frightened orphans into gurgles of laughter as he joked with them in fluent Vietnamese. Many a little boy, successfully treated for an eye infection, would return bearing an even smaller brother on his back for healing by the *Bac Sy My* (American Doctor).

Tom was not merely fighting starvation and disease. Many of his patients had suffered at the hands of the Viet Minh. Among then were women, children and old people, some of whom had been badly beaten up. Before he finally got away from Haiphong, Tom was himself arrested by the new Communist masters and held for a day and a night in a stinking cell while they questioned him, with courteous venom, about his rich American life-style: "Monsieur, is it not true that you own a car whose value equals the annual salary of many Vietnamese?"

Before that happened, however, he had seen for himself what these self-appointed champions of the poor were capable of.

Late one November night Tom was awakened at his hotel by a Vietnamese priest who asked him to see a patient urgently. Together the two men drove in a jeep to the outskirts of the city.

After many months of caring for his refugees Tom was used to heart-rendering sights. Nevertheless, the spectacle that now met his eyes filled him with horror.

The patient, an elderly priest in a Communist-held village, had been in his church when the Vietminh soldiers burst in and accused him of preaching lies about them. The priest told them that he spoke only of God.

The Communists took the old man, hung him from a beam by his feet and stripped him naked. They beat him with short bamboo rods, covering almost every inch and attacking the most sensitive areas with particular savagery. They rammed chopsticks deep into his ears. They dug thorns deep into his head, in mockery of the crown which Christ wore. When the altar-boys arrived in the morning he was still hanging there. The blood-vessels in his eyes had ruptured, leaving him nearly blind.

The youngsters knew that if the Viet Minh came again their priest would certainly be killed. They knew that they had to get him away. With incredible bravery and resourcefulness they carried the terribly injured man through the rice paddies to the river's edge—a journey lasting a day and a night. They dared not try to get him across the river in daylight, so they hid among the rushes until the next nightfall. Then they put the stretcher on to a wooden raft, pushed the raft across the fast-flowing current to the opposite bank, and carried the priest to the mission where the doctor found him. Amazingly, he recovered—thanks to Tom's care.

Another priest, also treated by Tom, had suffered even more cruelly. Not only had the Viet Minh destroyed his hearing, they had cut out his tongue with a rusty bayonet so that he could never again preach the word of God. With him were a group of children whom he had been teaching. Their eardrums, too, had been pierced so that they would never again listen to it. Yet another of Tom's priest-patients had had six nails driven into his head.

"Why are these atrocity cases always priests?" he asked later. "Why do they hate priests so—because they are so near the One they really hate?"

One of his last acts before leaving Vietnam was to rescue a five-foot statue of Our Lady of Fatima which stood above the altar of a church in Haiphong. Many years before it had been the Pope's gift to a group of Vietnamese pilgrims to Rome. Tom was determined that it should not fall into Communist hands. The poor, barefooted clergy sadly agreed to let him carry it to safety.

For his services to the refugees, Tom was personally decorated by South Vietnam's President Diem. His own country awarded him the Legion of Merit. Yet whatever Tom had done for the refugees, he felt that they had done much more for him. They had shown him where his life's work lay.

Once he had dreamed of becoming a fashionable obstetrician. Later on he imagined himself as Surgeon-General of the Navy and others, including the reigning Surgeon-General, also saw Tom as a future occupant of that post. Now all such ambitions were abandoned as Tom began to dream of a future devoted to the suffering people of South-east Asia.

On leave in Washington, he attended a party at the South Vietnamese Embassy. There he talked to his hosts about his plan for a small medical mission, independent of all governmental or political ties, to work in areas where there was no doctor. Diplomats from Cambodia and Laos were among the guests and Tom, as he talked, noticed that the Laotian Ambassador was following him keenly.

"Dr. Dooley," asked the Ambassador when he had finished, "why should you, a young man with your career before you, offer to make so great a sacrifice?"

Into Tom's mind came the words of a naval corpsman in Haiphong. Questioned about American motives, he had answered: "We just want to do what we can for people who ain't got it so good."

The simple words touched the Ambassador more than a hundred sentiments. A few days later, Tom told his mother: "I'm resigning from the Navy and I'm going to Laos."

Some of Tom's friends—people who thought they knew him

well—were astonished by his decision. Even his mother admitted that she was shocked. Yet she, above all others, knew the serious side of Tom's nature: the sense of responsibility which he had always felt towards his fellow-men. The whole family had been deeply affected by the death of Tom's older brother, Earle, in World War II. Before he was killed by a mortar shell, Earle had written a letter to his family charging them to do all in their power to fight against war and the things that led to war. Tom carried that letter with him constantly. His deepest motivation, however, came from his faith. Tom was a patriotic American and he wanted those whom he helped to think well of his country. Yet that help, he insisted again and again, must be without strings, political or religious. He did not seek to turn his patients into Republicans or Democrats; nor did he try to make them Catholics. He brought Christ to them, not by preaching but by devoting his life to their care.

Operation Laos, as Tom called his mission, began in July, 1956, at a village called Van Vieng, where he and his three ex-Navy helpers arrived covered in mud and red dust, looking like men in dire need of help rather than men come to give it. "For the many who had never seen an American," Tom recalled later, "I'm afraid we must have been something of a disenchantment."

Nevertheless the villagers gave them a warm welcome, and even the children pitched in to help them to prepare a hut standing on five-foot stilts as their living quarters. While washing and painting proceeded above, the village livestock—pigs, cows, chickens and ducks—scratched about underneath.

The hospital, where the 25 patients lay on mats, was housed in a dispensary owned by the Laotian government. Many more patients were treated in their own homes for malaria, pneumonia, malnutrition and beri-beri.

From the beginning, the International Rescue Committee took Operation Laos under its wing and Tom's energetic begging brought supplies from America's leading pharmaceutical companies. Walt Disney, meanwhile, donated a projector and a collection of his own films—a gift which proved invaluable in winning the confidence of youngsters.

Of Tom's hundreds of outpatients, many walked vast distances to tell their symptoms and to receive medicines, not from Tom himself but from the Lao assistants whom he had trained to do the dispensing. For Tom was more than a doctor, he was also an educator, and the American doctors who joined him were expected to fulfil the same role. "An Asian helping an Asian is better than an American helping an Asian," he would declare firmly, as he watched his pupils learn their basic skills. Many of them reached a high degree of proficiency in a surprisingly short space of time, rudimentary though their training was. Midwives qualified when they had assisted at 25 deliveries and completed a two-month course.

To the charge that he was practising nineteenth-century medicine, he pleaded guilty. Once he left, he told his critics cheerfully, his pupils might well revert to eighteenth-century medicine—but even that would be a gain for people who were living in the fifteenth century. Meanwhile he would listen with a mixture of pride and amusement as young men who a few months previously would not have known one end of a hypodermic from the other, discussed patients' symptoms with the aplomb of Mayo Clinic counsultants.

Some of those symptoms were horrible enough—although familiar to the Lao helpers, who had grown up from birth with the effects of starvation and disease all around them.

One day, for example, a group arrived at the clinic after a 100-mile walk, bringing with them a sickly-looking young mother who thrust a bundle of clothing under their noses. As Tom and his assistants unwrapped the bundle, layer upon layer of it, they found a child whose abdomen was so huge and distended that it looked as though it might burst at any moment, like an over-blown balloon. Around the child's navel were a dozen or so round brown marks where the local witch-doctor had burned the skin with pieces of hot ginger-root to draw the sickness out. Because she herself was ill, the mother had been unable to nurse the child so she fed it on rice-and-water. Soon it was suffering from beri-beri.

Even after his arrival, the power of the witch-doctor remained great, for the beliefs of centuries are not upset in a day. Tom soon learned to treat these ladies and gentlemen as professional colleagues. When he called he would first gravely stir the pot in which the all-powerful potation, liberally seasoned with incantations, was bubbling. Having thus established a rapport, he would settle himself to discuss the patient's condition. It was tacitly agreed that any credit for a cure must be equally shared between Eastern and Western medicine. Any eggs or other produce received by way of fees were likewise divided.

This policy of cooperation paid a hundredfold dividend. Frequently Tom would be called in when the witch-doctor had failed, sometimes at short notice. Once he arrived by jeep, having been wakened at 3 a.m., to find a man in his early forties suffering from pneumonia and close to death. Tom put him on an improvised stretcher, raised the lower part of his body and constructed a crude vaporiser from a fire-pot, an old blanket and a length of bamboo attached to a tea-kettle. As one of his American helpers commented later: "That was nineteenth-century medicine all right, but it saved that man's life."

Even though he had to practise medicine in primitive conditions, Tom would tolerate no relaxation of standards in any of his hospitals. No matter how trying the circumstances, maximum hygiene had to be observed. An American assistant who arrived in the operating theatre minus cap and gown got a sharp dressing-down, even though he felt that he had a legitimate excuse. Soon afterwards, Tom presented him with a length of material and told him to have himself a cap and gown made forthwith.

Episodes like this naturally helped to give Tom his reputation for arrogance. The truth was that he had no patience with laxity, or anything that seemed like it. That his style was autocratic cannot be denied; no doubt his service background was largely responsible for that. "You must give the orders and they must obey," he told an American colleague whom he thought too much inclined to consult his subordinates.

He demanded total sacrifice from himself and he also demanded it from others. "If there are any emergency calls in the night I'll wake you and you can drive me," he told another helper. As the man later observed wryly: "It would never occur to him to *ask*."

Yet with his patients he was always the soul of courtesy. An elderly whisky-seller, whom he had treated for tuberculosis, spotted Tom and an American colleague as they walked through the market-place. Tom stopped to chat and the old man offered each of them a drink of his unspeakable local brew from a common cup which must have been riddled with disease-laden bacteria.

Tom, whose favorite drink was bourbon, drank without flickering an eyelid and thanked the donor politely. When his companion queasily tried to decline the liquor, Tom dug him in the ribs.

"Drink it, you fool!" he hissed. "You can't offend his hospitality!"

When he established Medico in 1956, Tom was already famous, thanks to his published account of the Vietnamese evacuation, *Deliver Us From Evil*. He received thousands of letters from well-wishers, especially after *Reader's Digest* ran a condensation. As his fame grew, discussions of Tom's shortcomings, real or alleged, became public—part of his cross during the few years that were left to him.

Those who called him a phoney, out for his own self-glorification, hurt him deeply. Because he was so forceful few realised that he was a sensitive man—and he hid it well.

"What do you get out of this deal, Dooley?" a brash reporter asked him.

"Plenty," Tom replied evenly. "My life is more worth-while."

Tom *was* an unabashed publicity-seeker, not because he wanted people to admire him, but because he knew that the books, lecture tours and news stories brought him the dollars and the volunteers that he needed to maintain and extend his work. Yet he recoiled from any attempt to put him on a pedestal.

"People keep trying to make me into a St. Francis," he growled as his fame grew. "It's gotten so that I can't walk into a bar and have a beer."

When villagers kow-towed before him on the roads of Laos, Tom would immediately raise them up.

"Don't worship me or anyone else—worship God!" he would tell them. "You're as good as I am. You're as good as anyone in the world."

He got really cross when Medico's New York headquarters proposed that he should have his own personally-headed notepaper. "Whoever thought that one up ought to go and stand in the corner," he snorted. "I don't care how you people in New York use my name, so long as you are sure it helps Medico. But let's not get silly."

Medico grew naturally out of Tom's work at Van Vieng. As support gathered in volume it became possible to realise his dream of an organization which would send medical teams like his own to deprived areas throughout the world. "International Medical Cooperation" was the phrase in Tom's head and this was quickly shortened to give the new organization its name.

Conscious of his own limitations, Tom did not make himself its administrative head. Anyway, he wanted to remain in Laos. Dr. Peter Comanduras, a medical man with the right kind of experience, was appointed to head Medico in New York and an advisory board of distinguished doctors was set up.

Among those who sent their good wishes was Dr. Albert Schweitzer, who had done much to inspire Tom orginally. A short time before, he had visited Schweitzer at his hospital in Lambarené.

With Medico safely launched, Tom returned with a glad heart to Laos. He based himself now at Muong Sing, in the far north of the country, where Laos, China and Burma meet.

Though Medico opened other hospitals in Laos, Muong Sing was the one he made his own. Already the Chinese radio stations were broadcasting regular denunciations of Dooley the capitalist agent, but Tom did not worry about that. Instead he rejoiced in the name his patients gave him—*Thanh Mo America*. Literally, this means "Respectful Man of Medicine from America."

One of the Americans who joined him there, Earl Rhine, had a flair for dentistry. He got the even more colorful name *Thanh Mo Chep Keo*—"Respectful Man of Medicine for Pain in Teeth."

Earl and his friend, Dwight Davies, left their young wives and their studies at the University of Texas to give Medico a piece of their lives. Despite his self-proclaimed faults, Tom attracted many other idealistic young people to his side. Most became personally devoted to him as well as to the work.

The first encounter could be daunting: a young man who had never been east of Oklahoma might be summoned to meet Tom in a New York hotel the following day. The fact that he had some prior commitment, or did not possess the fare, was not accepted as an excuse. When he was up against it in some jungle village, the youngster would need self-sacrifice and resourcefulness in plenty. If he got to the appointment on time, he had passed the first test.

Whether Tom saw the applicant personally or not, he always had his background checked out thoroughly. In particular he was wary of taking on anyone whose motives might be suspect. One man he did interview was a young Catholic who, having realised that he did not have the vocation, had recently given up his studies for the priesthood.

With this candidate Tom was almost cruel. He openly accused him of wanting to go to Asia in order to turn Buddhists into Catholics, and so compensate himself for not becoming a priest. So abrasive was the grilling that the young man grew white with anger. Nevertheless he refused to lose his temper and he stuck to his guns. His motive, he insisted, was the same as Tom's own. He simply wanted to help the people who "didn't have it so good".

In fact the whole interview was simply another Dooley test. Having come through it with flying colors, the ex-seminarian was duly appointed to Medico. He proved a first-rate field worker. When he made up his mind to accept someone, Tom did not waste time on formalities. "Okay, you leave next month," he would say. "You will work at _____. Get a map and look it up."

Many of the volunteers were doctors or had some other qualification. Others, like Earl and Dwight, went on to study medicine when their stint with Medico was complete. For these, the work which they were doing offered a range of experience which they could scarcely have found anywhere else. Leprosy and smallpox, diseases long banished from the West, were part of the everyday scene. Diphtheria, whooping-cough and typhoid, well known to earlier generations of U.S. doctors, were still alive and flourishing in the villages of Laos.

Intricate surgery was practised in the humblest of operating-rooms. More than once Tom had to perform plastic surgery on youngsters horribly disfigured in attacks from wild bears. One lad had his left eye and the bridge of his nose torn off. Tom had to do his best with the ribbons of flesh that were left.

Another small patient, similarly patched up, presented the surprised surgeon with a little dog as a token of his appreciation. Thanking him, Tom asked smilingly: "What can I do with it?"

It was the boy's turn to look surprised. "Eat it," he replied.

Though Tom enjoyed seeing his family on visits to the States, he was always eager to get back to his patients once the lectures had been delivered and the conferences with Medico staff completed. Only in Laos was he completely happy.

In his book *The Night They Burned the Mountain* Tom has himself described how he first got the news of his fatal cancer. A soldier walked into the hospital at Muong Sing and announced that a telegram awaited him at the fortress. Since it had come via military radio, Tom's first thought was that it concerned the war. Communist troops were massing on the border and some reports said they were already in Laos.

The telegram was from Dr. Comanduras, Medico's director, recalling him to New York immediately. Even then, Tom did not suspect that his own health was involved. Had something happened to his mother, he wondered. Or was there some crisis within Medico itself?

In Vientiane, on the journey home, someone suggested that he was required to appear in a TV show. If that proved true, Tom replied, he would use language on the air that would close TV down for ever. War casualties might arrive in Muong Sing at any moment. Didn't Peter Comanduras realise that his place was in his hospital?

In fact, Tom's closest associates already knew the truth, and it was one of these who broke it to him as he passed through Bangkok. The words, said Tom, made no impact on him whatever. They entered his head like a fist jammed into a pillow.

When Tom landed in New York and phoned his mother with the news she also could not absorb it at first. She felt confident that with rest and care, her son would soon be well again.

Round his neck Tom had for years worn a St. Christopher medal, engraved with some lines from a poem by Robert Frost:

> *The woods are lovely, dark and deep,*
> *But I have promises to keep,*
> *And miles to go before I sleep.*

Upon these words he had built his life. Now they had a magnificent urgency. He set himself to live them as never before.

Far from giving in to his condition, he redoubled his activities, travelling the world to extend the work of Medico to as many places on the map as possible, caring for his patients back in Laos.

First, however, Tom had a task to perform in New York. He had reacted acidly when his friend in Vientiane suggested that he was to appear on TV. Yet now he *did* appear on TV, in a program which made history. For the first time, millions of viewers heard a cancer patient talk about his operation—then they saw him having it.

By the time the program was screened, on April 21, 1960, Tom was back in Southeast Asia. In his room at Memorial Hospital, Tom admitted to the CBS reporter, Howard K. Smith, that his condition caused him some discomfiture—he rejected the word "pain" as being too strong. When Smith suggested that he was treating his situation in a way that was almost blithe, Tom replied: "I don't want any of that 'dying doctor's agony' stuff. That's stupid."

He welcomed the cameras, he explained, because in America there was a great deal of ignorance about cancer—much the same sort of ignorance as existed in his village in Laos. Patients were crippled by fear before ever they got into hospital and that handicapped their treatment straight away. He wanted to make people see that they need not be so afraid of cancer as they had been in the past.

Tom spoke to the camera as fluently and encouragingly as though it were a patient in Muong Sing, reaching out especially to people who might be suffering like himself. As one of the technicians put it, he was a "natural".

The viewers saw two operations. The first, which was exploratory, showed that the cancer had not spread as far as had been feared. In the second the surgeons cut out the cancerous tissue. So far as it went this operation was successful and Tom left the hospital ten days later. But he knew, as did everyone else, that the cancer could already be spreading through his bloodstream and growing in tiny spots in his lungs or liver or other vital organs. In fact that was what happened.

Meanwhile, Tom had his promises to keep. No sooner was he on his feet than he set off round America on a fund-raising tour, and the audiences who listened to him soon saw that illness had done little to dent his humor. In St. Louis, his home town, he had doctors roaring with laughter at his sly comparison between the non-committal grunts of a Lao witch-doctor and those of an American consultant, when faced with a patient whose condition they could not diagnose.

Christmas found him, loaded with gifts, back at Muong Sing. Every one of the village children got his own individually wrapped present. Tom was happy to find everyone safe and sound. During his absence in the States he had been anxious lest the Communists over-run the hospital, for he knew the likely fate of those of his colleagues whom they caught. The Americans would be publicly beheaded and their heads stuck on poles; the Lao workers would be hacked to death.

On New Year's Eve he wrote Peter Comanduras in New York: "I feel okay, but I know I'm not the same Dooley I was a year ago . . ." A young doctor must be found, he said, to take over at Muong Sing in case he himself could not return after his next medical check-up in May.

The check-up, when it came, gave no indication that the melanoma was still present and this, coupled with Tom's amazing energy, gave some people false hopes. Even some of his doctor friends actually let themselves believe that he had the cancer beaten. Tom himself indulged in no such wishful thinking. He knew full well that a satisfactory report, so soon after his operation, meant little.

During 1960 he visited Burma, Vietnam, Afghanistan, Malaya, India, Hong Kong and Cambodia. In each country he did the groundwork for new Medico projects. He visited Teheran and several European capitals as well—London, Paris and Rome. At a private audience, Pope John emptied his desk-drawer of medals and rosaries and gave them to the dying young American of whom he had heard so much. In Rome, also, he was made a member of the Oblates of Mary Immaculate—a rare honor for a layman.

"If this guy's ill, I'd sure hate to follow him round when he's well!" said one of those who accompanied Tom at this time. And indeed his reserves of energy seemed inexhaustible.

Back in the States he received an honorary degree from his

own university, Notre Dame. Among others being honored was President Dwight D. Eisenhower.

As they donned their robes in the locker-room, Tom asked Ike to give his brother Malcolm a lift back to New York on board the Presidential plane. Malcolm was, he explained, an executive at Medico's New York headquarters, a busy man who had to get back to his desk. In fact this was pure Dooley chutzpah—Tom really wanted Malcolm to be able to tell to his grandchildren about the day he flew home with the President. Ike readily obliged, and an astonished Malcolm Dooley found himself being whisked away from his wife and family by secret servicemen and hustled into a car in the Presidential motorcade.

The time came, however, when Tom could no longer keep up his facade of high spirits. Forced to rest in a Hong Kong hospital, he looked at his X-ray plates and saw that the cancer had spread to his spine. "And I still have so much to do!" he lamented.

He returned once more to Muong Sing, but this time he was not to see another Christmas there. Christmas Day, 1960, found Tom in Bangkok, lying pain-racked on a mattress on the floor of his hotel room. He badly wanted to go to Midnight Mass at Holy Redeemer Church, but was too ill to make it. So Redemptorist Father John Boucher brought him Holy Communion instead.

When news of Tom's illness broke, one of the friends who had been with him in Laos declared bitterly: "There are thousands of jerks in the world we could do without. Why does someone like Tom Dooley have to get cancer?"

Yet this was never Tom's attitude. He did not complain, or ask, "Why me?" As he lay in his hotel room on that Christmas Day, he told Father Boucher, "If this is the way God wants it to be, this is the way I want it too." His suffering, he was convinced, had been sent for a purpose.

During the car journey from Idlewild to the Memorial Hospital he asked Teresa Gallagher, a devoted aide, to remind him to write and thank a stewardess who had been kind to him on the last, agonising leg of the flight, between London and New York, when he could neither stand, sit nor lie down without pain.

On Tuesday, January 17th, his birthday, Cardinal Spellman visited him in Room 910—the room from which he had made his television appearance. Tom, though sinking fast, recognised the cardinal and rose up in bed to make the Lao sign of greeting, head bowed and hands clasped before his face.

When he came out, the cardinal had tears in his eyes. "I tried to assure him that in his 34 years he had done what very few have done in the allotted Scriptural lifetime," he said.

At 9.45 p.m. on the following day, Tom Dooley died, quietly and peacefully, his promises kept.

Bibliography

Charles de Foucauld, by Margaret Trouncer. Harrap, London, 1972.

The Desert My Dwelling Place, by Elizabeth Hamilton. Hodder and Stoughton, London, 1968.

Pilgrimage to God: The Spirit of Charles de Foucauld, by A Little Brother of Jesus. Translated by Jeremy Moiser. Darton, Longman and Todd, London, 1974.

Memories of Charles de Foucauld, by Georges Gorrée. Translated by Donald Attwater. Burns, Oates and Washbourne, London, 1938.

The Man Who Got Even With God, by M. Raymond, OCSO. Clonmore and Reynolds, Dublin, 1954.

Matt Talbot, by Eddie Doherty. Bruce Publishing Co., Milwaukee, 1953.

Father Miguel Pro, SJ, by Fanchon Royer. Clonmore and Reynolds, Dublin, 1955.

Many Mexicos, by L. B. Simpson. University of California Press, Berkeley and Los Angeles, 1966.

The Lawless Roads, by Graham Greene. Longmans Green and Co., London, 1939.

Brother Andre of Mount Royal, by Katherine Burton. Clonmore and Reynolds, Dublin, 1955.

Edel Quinn, by L-J. Suenens. Fallon, Dublin, 1954.

Father Vincent McNabb, OP, by Ferdinand Valentine, OP. Burns and Oates, London, 1955.

A Saint in Hyde Park, by E. A. Siderman. Geoffrey Bles, London, 1950.

The Journeying Ladies, by Joyce Sugg. Burns and Oates, London, 1967.

The Scholar and the Cross, by Hilda C. Graef. Longmans Green, London, 1955.

Walls Are Crumbling, by John M. Oesterreicher. Hollis and Carter, London, 1953.

Titus Brandsma, A Modern Martyr, by Joseph Rees. Sidgwick and Jackson, London, 1971.

Bakhita, Pearl of the Sudan, by Aloysius Roche. St. Paul Publications, Langley, Bucks., 1968.

Deliver Us From Evil, by Thomas A. Dooley. Farrar, Strauss and Cudahy, New York, 1956.

The Edge of Tomorrow, by Thomas A. Dooley. Farrar, Strauss and Cudahy, New York, 1958.

The Night They Burned the Mountain, by Thomas A. Dooley. Farrar, Strauss and Cudahy, New York, 1960.

Promises To Keep, by Agnes W. Dooley. Farrar, Strauss and Cudahy, New York, 1962.

Before I Sleep, by James Monahan. Farrar, Strauss and Cudahy, New York, 1961.